Navigating Washington D.C. Like a Pro: Insider Secrets for Success in America's Capital

JAYEEL MUNCH

ISBN: 9798875979002

DEDICATION

To those who explore Washington D.C.,
a global capital of the world

CONTENTS

ACKNOWLEDGMENTS

I extend my heartfelt gratitude to all those who contributed to the creation of this book. This endeavor would not have been possible without the support, encouragement, and expertise of them.

INTRODUCTION

In 1842, Charles Dickens, the esteemed British novelist and literary figure, embarked on a journey to the United States and chronicled his experiences in the travelogue "American Notes for General Circulation." In this work, Dickens aptly labeled Washington as the "City of Magnificent Intentions."

> *Spacious avenues, that begin in nothing, and lead nowhere; streets, mile-long, that only want houses, roads and inhabitants; public buildings that need but a public to be complete; and ornaments of great thoroughfares, which only lack great thoroughfares to ornament—are its leading features. One might fancy the season over, and most of the houses gone out of town for ever with their masters. To the admirers of cities it is a Barmecide Feast: a pleasant field for the imagination to rove in; a monument raised to a deceased project, with not even a legible inscription to record its departed greatness.*
>
> *Charles Dickens, "American Notes for General Circulation"*

Washington D.C. (hereinafter referred to as Washington) is known for its unique blend of historical tradition and modernity. Since being designated as the capital of the United States only 230 years ago, the city is filled with landmarks and architecture that exude a sense of compact tradition. Over the years, politicians and residents alike have made conscious efforts to preserve the city's historic charm, giving it the appearance of an older, more traditional city.

One such example of this effort is evident in the city's architecture, particularly in its federal buildings such as the White House, Eisenhower Executive Office Building, and Supreme Court. These structures were constructed in the neoclassical style, which was popular during the late 18th and early 19th centuries, and draws inspiration from the classical Greek and Roman architecture that dates back over 2,000 years.

In a city with a young history, those with deep roots and long memories are highly valued. The political landscape of the city is in a constant state of flux, with changes in governance occurring every few years, frequent elections for lawmakers and their staff, and foreign diplomats and international organizations' employees being posted for relatively brief periods.

In this fast-paced and ever-changing environment, having a

broad network of connections and a deep understanding of the city's inner workings can be the key to success in any profession. Whether you are a politician, a businessperson, or a resident, building meaningful relationships and staying up to date on the latest happenings in the city is essential for achieving your goals.

This book aims to familiarize readers with every facet of Washington. Through an exploration of its rich history, notable landmarks, important networks, and vibrant dining scenes, you'll be well-equipped to build a successful career in this bustling cosmopolitan center.

In the upcoming chapter, *A Short History of Washington*, we unravel the rich tapestry of Washington's history. From its early days as a fledgling capital to the defining moments that shaped its identity, this chapter serves as a compelling narrative, painting a vivid picture of the city's evolution. As you delve into its historical depths, you'll gain insights into the forces that have molded Washington into the iconic capital it is today.

Navigate the visual landscape of Washington in the chapter, *A Brief Optics of Washington Map,* as we dissect the city through a unique lens. This chapter is your visual guide, highlighting key districts, landmarks, and the intricate network that weaves through its urban fabric. By understanding the geography, you'll gain a clearer perspective on the layout of the capital, enhancing your ability to traverse its streets and explore its hidden gems.

In *Washington Institutions You Can't Afford to Miss*, we delve into the very heartbeat of the nation's capital – its institutions. From political powerhouses to think tanks, these institutions play a pivotal role in shaping the city's character. Whether you're a visitor seeking to absorb the city's essence or a professional aiming to make an impact, this chapter provides a guide to the must-see institutions that define Washington.

Begin your professional culinary exploration in *Finding the Professional Dining Experience in Washington*, where we dive into the dining experiences that characterize Washington's gastronomic scene. Beyond satisfying hunger, these dining spots serve as hubs for networking and leisure. Discover the flavors that define the city and learn how dining experiences can be integral to both professional and personal connections in this bustling metropolis.

As you plan your stay in Washington, *Exploring Accommodation Options in Washington* is your guide to navigating the varied landscape of accommodations. From sleek urban apartments to historic neighborhoods, this chapter explores options that not only provide comfort but also align with your professional pursuits. Your residence in the city becomes a key element in your experience, and this chapter ensures you make an informed choice.

The next chapter, *Washington's Cultural Tapestry: Art, Music, and Theater Scene* unfolds as a vivid exploration of the capital's vibrant artistic and creative landscape. From the grand halls of the Kennedy Center to the intimate settings of legendary jazz clubs, this chapter delves into the captivating world of the performing arts, showcasing the diverse influences that shape Washington's cultural identity.

The forthcoming chapters, *Washington Lingo* and *Washington in Movies and TV Shows*, explore the linguistic and visual dimensions originating from the capital of the United States. In *Washington Lingo*, readers will delve into a lexicon that not only conveys the intricacies of policymaking but also mirrors the distinctive culture and influence that define the city.

On the cinematic canvas, *Washington in Movies and TV Shows* casts a spotlight on portrayals that have etched an enduring mark on our collective consciousness. These chapters unravel the grandeur of iconic landmarks, untangle political dramas, and pulse with the vibrant rhythm of life within the city. Together, these chapters offer a comprehensive exploration of the words, expressions, and images that emanate from the heart of the nation, providing readers with a nuanced understanding of Washington's linguistic and cinematic identity.

Exploring *Transportation in Washington* unveils a wealth of local knowledge on navigating the city—guiding readers on how, when, and where to move seamlessly. Washington stands out as a city without a singular dominant mode of transportation, presenting a hybrid array of options that enrich the reader's understanding of the city's mobility landscape. This diverse spectrum of transportation choices becomes an invaluable source of learning, offering insights into the dynamic ways in which residents and visitors can traverse and connect within the vibrant tapestry of Washington.

The final chapter, *Additional Tips for Your Quick Settlement*, serves as your comprehensive toolkit for settling into the rhythm of daily life in Washington. Offering practical insights and advice, this chapter covers everything from local customs to essential services, ensuring that your settlement in the vibrant capital is smooth and efficient.

Embark on this insightful journey through the chapters, and let this guide be your companion in unraveling the complexities and delights of Washington. Whether you're here for professional pursuits or seeking to immerse yourself in the city's cultural tapestry, this exploration promises to enrich your experience in the iconic capital. After reading it, you'll be equipped to hit the ground running in Washington, regardless of your job. You'll be living proof of the city's status as the capital of the United States.

A SHORT HISTORY OF WASHINGTON

Washington, D.C., formally known as the District of Columbia, was established as the capital of the United States in 1790. Prior to its founding, the United States did not have a permanent capital city, and Congress would meet in various locations, including New York City and Philadelphia.

The idea of a new capital was proposed by Alexander Hamilton, who envisioned a central location that would be independent of any individual state. The location chosen for the new capital was a 100-square-mile area on the Potomac River, which was donated by the states of Maryland and Virginia.

The city was designed by French architect Pierre Charles L'Enfant, who came to America from France to fight in the Revolutionary War and envisioned a grand capital with wide avenues and public squares. Construction of the city began in 1791, and by 1800, the federal government had moved to Washington.

In 1814, during the War of 1812, British forces invaded Washington and burned down many important government buildings, including the White House and the Capitol. This event is now known as the Burning of Washington. Despite this setback, the city was rebuilt and continued to grow as a political and cultural hub.

During the Civil War (1861-1865), Washington was an important center of military operations for the Union Army. Many battles were fought in and around the city, and the city also became a refuge for escaped slaves. After the Civil War, Washington became a hub of political activity as Congress worked to rebuild the nation and ensure civil rights for all citizens. This period, known as Reconstruction, saw the passage of the 13th, 14th, and 15th Amendments to the U.S. Constitution, which abolished slavery, granted citizenship to former slaves, and ensured the right to vote regardless of race.

During both World War I and World War II, Washington was an important center of military planning and strategy. The city played a significant role in the Allied victory in both conflicts. In addition to military efforts, Washington played a role in promoting peace and diplomacy. In 1945, the United Nations was founded in San Francisco, but the headquarters was established in New York City with a branch office in Washington

In the 1950s and 1960s, Washington became a focal point of the Civil Rights Movement. Activists marched on the National Mall and lobbied Congress for equal rights and an end to segregation. This period of time is characterized by many historical events, such as the March on Washington in 1963 where Martin Luther King Jr. delivered his "I Have a Dream" speech. In 1964, the Civil Rights Act was signed into law, prohibiting discrimination based on race, color, religion, sex, or national origin.

In recent decades, Washington has continued to be a center of political activity, home to the White House, Congress, and many other important government institutions. The city has also seen significant growth and development, with new museums, restaurants, and cultural attractions opening regularly. The city has faced challenges, such as the 9/11 terrorist attacks in 2001, which had a significant impact on national security and the city's landscape. However,

Washington has remained a symbol of democracy and freedom, attracting visitors from all over the world to witness the rich history and culture of the nation's capital.

In addition to its historical significance and cultural richness, Washington became a focal point for Black Lives Matter (BLM) protests in recent years. Following the killing of George Floyd in Minneapolis in May 2020, the movement gained momentum across the United States, including in the nation's capital. Thousands of protesters gathered in Washington to demand an end to police brutality, systemic racism, and social injustice. The streets near the White House and the National Mall witnessed a surge of passionate demonstrators advocating for racial equality and police reform.

These protests in Washington were marked by both peaceful demonstrations and instances of confrontation between protesters and law enforcement. The Lafayette Square, located near the White House, gained particular attention as a site where protesters were forcefully dispersed to make way for President Donald Trump's photo opportunity at St. John's Church. The clash between protesters and law enforcement, along with the use of tear gas and rubber bullets, drew widespread criticism and ignited a national conversation on the militarization of the police and the right to peaceful assembly. The BLM protests in Washington not only highlighted the urgent need for racial justice but also sparked debates on the role of law enforcement and the protection of civil liberties in the nation's capital.

Despite the challenges and controversies surrounding the protests, they also led to tangible changes in Washington. The local government, under Mayor Muriel Bowser, painted the words "Black Lives Matter" on a section of 16th Street near the White House, transforming it into a visual symbol of solidarity with the movement. The protests played a crucial role in pushing for legislative changes and fostering a national dialogue on racial inequality. Washington, as the political epicenter of the United States, became a prominent stage for this important chapter in the ongoing struggle for racial justice.

Over the years, Washington has been the site of many important events in American history, including the Civil War and the civil rights movement. It has also been the location of many important government buildings and monuments, including the White House, the Capitol Building, and the Lincoln Memorial.

Today, Washington is a thriving city with a diverse population and a rich cultural heritage. It remains an important center of political power and is home to many museums, galleries, and other cultural institutions. Additionally, the city is also home to several professional sports teams, including the Washington Football Team (NFL), Washington Nationals (MLB), Washington Capitals (NHL), Washington Wizards (NBA), and DC United (MLS). These teams have a passionate following among the city's residents and help to make Washington a vibrant and exciting place to live and visit.

Despite Washington's thriving and diverse community, it has long been plagued by a significant political grievance: the city has no voting rights in Congress and no representation in the Senate. Although residents of the capital city pay federal taxes and serve in the military, they are not afforded the same democratic rights as citizens of the fifty states.

Efforts to grant Washington statehood and full voting rights have been ongoing for decades, with supporters arguing that it is a matter of basic democratic principles. However, progress has been slow, with political polarization and opposition from some lawmakers preventing significant action on the issue.

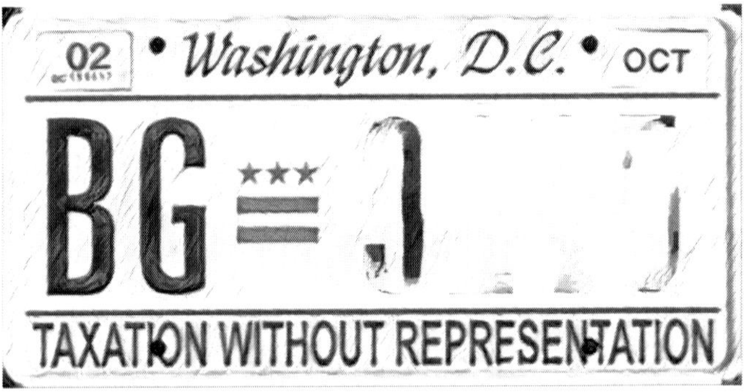

In recent years, there has been renewed momentum and support for granting statehood to Washington This shift in the political landscape has generated hope among many residents of the capital city that they will one day have full representation in Congress and a voice in presidential elections. Despite ongoing obstacles, advocates for D.C. statehood remain committed to their cause. If the city were to achieve statehood, it would finally gain the political rights and representation that its residents have been fighting for, and the car plate motto "End Taxation Without Representation" would become a thing of the past.

A BRIEF OPTICS OF WASHINGTON MAP

Embarking on an in-depth examination of the map of Washington invites us to delve beyond the surface and uncover the intricate layers of history, design, and deliberate planning that have shaped the capital into the dynamic city it is today.

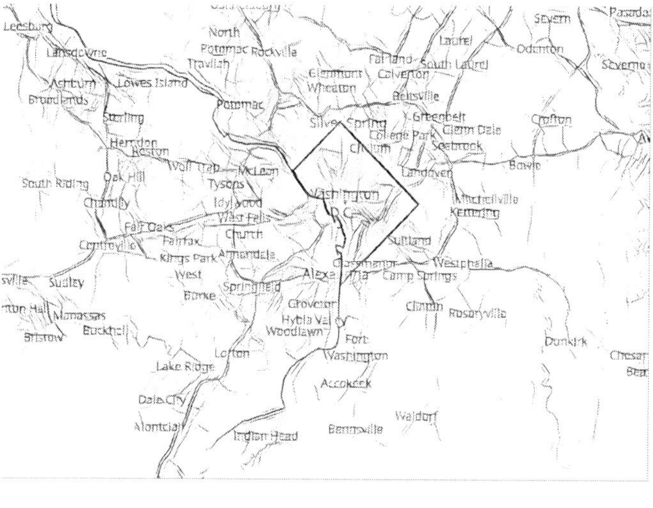

To begin with, what are your initial thoughts on the current map of Washington? Does it appear to be a well-planned city? The city's shape, resembling a broken diamond, may suggest otherwise. Interestingly, it was originally designed as a complete diamond shape before undergoing changes.

The Broken Diamond Shape: Unraveling Washington's Evolution

As we gaze upon the city's map, the peculiar broken diamond shape may ignite curiosity about its origins and the forces that led to its distinctive form. Initially conceived as a complete diamond, Washington underwent a transformative shift in 1864 with the passage of the "retrocession" act by the U.S. Congress. This legislative act, returning a portion of land to Virginia, was a pivotal moment in the city's history, altering its rhombus shape.

Contrary to a common misconception, Washington did not lose territory to Virginia. Instead, a segment of land known as Alexandria County, encompassing present-day Alexandria and Arlington, was retroceded back to Virginia in 1847. Motivated by the residents' desire to reunite with Virginia and concerns about the District's financial well-being, this move shaped the broken diamond silhouette we see today. Arlington County, as it is known today, hosts significant government institutions, including the Pentagon and Arlington National Cemetery.

The relationship between Washington and Virginia transcends mere geographic proximity. It is a complex tapestry woven from economic interdependence, historical ties, and shared cultural institutions. Yet, like any intricate fabric, it bears the marks of wear and tear, revealing areas of friction alongside enduring strengths.

On the one hand, Virginia serves as a crucial supply chain

for the District's workforce. Commuting residents contribute significantly to Washington's economic dynamism, while the proximity of government institutions and cultural magnets like museums and national landmarks provides Virginia with access to a vibrant and diverse environment. Collaborative efforts on regional challenges like transportation infrastructure and environmental protection further underscore the interconnectedness of their fates.

However, the relationship is not without its tensions. Issues such as commuting frustrations and the rising cost of living in Virginia, driven in part by the demand from Washington workers, generate discontent amongst some Virginians. Political polarization exacerbates these fissures, as policy disagreements between the District's predominantly Democratic populace and Virginia's more diverse political landscape can lead to gridlock and resentment. Furthermore, the limited powers of D.C. law enforcement beyond its borders, exemplified by the ongoing debate over enforcing speeding tickets on Virginia residents, create practical challenges that fuel these underlying frictions.

The recent Amazon HQ2 decision, initially perceived as a joint triumph, has also begun to reveal potential sources of tension. Concerns regarding gentrification and uneven economic distribution associated with the project highlight the inherent complexities of balancing regional development with individual community concerns.

Despite these challenges, the Washington-Virginia symbiosis remains undeniably strong. Shared history, economic dependence, and the need for mutual cooperation on critical issues continue to bind the two entities together. While navigating this intertwined relationship isn't always smooth sailing, its enduring nature suggests that both parties will continue to work towards an equilibrium that balances individual needs with a shared vision for the future.

Layout Design: A Symphony of Symbolism and Functionality

Washington was designed to be a symbolic representation of the newly-formed United States, with grand avenues, public spaces, and monumental buildings that reflected the aspirations and ideals of the young nation. The design was heavily influenced by European city planning principles, particularly the Baroque and Neoclassical styles of Paris and Rome.

Washington is divided into four administrative quadrants: Northeast (NE), Northwest (NW), Southeast (SE), and Southwest (SW). The dividing lines for these quadrants are centered around the Capitol Hill area of the city. The National Mall and East Capitol Street serve as the north-south demarcation line, while North Capitol Street and South Capitol Street function as the east-west dividing lines. The quadrants are essential for identifying locations and addresses in the city and are also utilized by city government organizations and emergency services for administrative and logistical purposes. Alongside the quadrants, Washington is segregated into eight wards, each of which has an elected council member representing the ward's inhabitants in the city council.

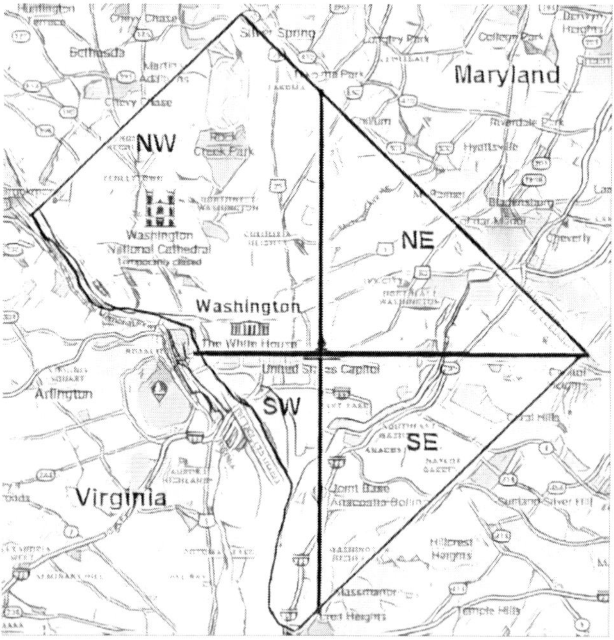

The city streets follow three primary directions: east-west, north-south, and diagonal. East-west streets are named with letters, north-south streets are numbered, and the diagonal streets are named after states. This logical and systematic approach to street naming facilitates navigation and reflects the city's well-organized layout.

The idea of incorporating states into the street names is more evident in the city's avenues, which radiate out from the Capitol building. These broad thoroughfares are named after states, serving as a way to honor and recognize the country's diverse regions. Examples include Massachusetts Avenue, New York Avenue, and Connecticut Avenue. However, not all 50 states are represented, and the selection of states for the avenue names doesn't necessarily follow a strict alphabetical or geographical order.

Additionally, some neighborhoods in Washington have streets named after prominent figures associated with specific states, indirectly linking certain streets to the states themselves. For example, streets in the Foggy Bottom neighborhood, near the George Washington University campus, are named after U.S. presidents, including those from different states. While the city's street naming system may not comprehensively incorporate all 50 states, the influence of states is subtly woven into the fabric of Washington's urban landscape.

Capitol Hill: The Pinnacle of Purposeful Design

At the heart of Washington's meticulous layout lies Capitol Hill, strategically positioned on an elevated site for an unparalleled view of the Potomac River. Departing from conventional practices, the Capitol was intentionally chosen as the focal point, giving rise to Capitol Hill as the vibrant central hub of the city.

This intentional design extends to the network of diagonal avenues radiating from Capitol Hill, intersecting the grid street system. Beyond facilitating transportation, these expansive boulevards offer enchanting vistas of landmarks and squares from considerable distances. To strike a balance between urban development and green spaces, public squares and parks were thoughtfully woven into key intersections, enhancing both the aesthetic charm and functional appeal of the city's design.

Monumental Vistas

The Axial Design and Symbolic Alignment: At the heart of the city's design lies the National Mall's axial layout, carefully aligning key monuments to reflect a balanced and united government. The Capitol Building anchors one end, symbolizing legislative power, while the Washington Monument stands tall at the other, paying homage to the nation's first president. This axial design serves as a powerful representation of the Founding Fathers' vision for a harmonious and balanced democracy.

The Washington Monument: Our exploration begins with the towering Washington Monument, a tribute to George Washington. Delve into its construction, architectural symbolism, and the panoramic views it offers from its observation deck. Learn about the profound impact of this iconic structure on the city's skyline and its enduring significance as a symbol of the nation's unity.

Lincoln Memorial and Reflecting Pool: Moving along the National Mall, we arrive at the Lincoln Memorial, a solemn tribute to Abraham Lincoln. Explore the memorial's historical and architectural significance, emphasizing the alignment with the Reflecting Pool. Discover how the statue of Lincoln, seated in contemplation, embodies the ideals of unity and equality, creating a poignant space for reflection.

Jefferson Memorial and Tidal Basin: Our journey continues to the Jefferson Memorial, gracefully situated along the Tidal Basin. Uncover the memorial's design and the symbolic homage it pays to Thomas Jefferson, the principal author of the Declaration of Independence. As we explore the serene beauty of this location, we gain insights into the ideals of democracy and enlightenment that shaped the nation's foundation.

Honoring Sacrifice: Vietnam Veterans, Korean War Veterans, and more: Our exploration concludes with a visit to the solemn memorials dedicated to those who served in the Vietnam War, the Korean War, and World War II. Delve into the emotional impact of these memorials, each with unique designs that capture the sacrifices made by servicemen and women. From the poignant symbolism of the Vietnam Veterans Memorial to the grandeur of the World War II Memorial, we reflect on the collective history and heroism encapsulated within these hallowed grounds.

WASHINGTON INSTITUTIONS YOU CAN'T AFFORD TO MISS

No matter how long you plan to stay in Washington and what type of work you do, whether it be for government, embassies, multinational companies, or international organizations, there are certain places and institutions that you should be familiar with in order to work efficiently in the city. Without this knowledge, you may not be able to perform your job at a professional level in Washington.

White House

The White House is the official residence and workplace of the President of the United States, making it one of the most iconic and significant buildings in the world. Located at 1600 Pennsylvania Avenue NW in Washington, the White House serves as the primary residence and workplace for the President and the First Family.

The construction of the White House began in 1792, and President John Adams became the first occupant in 1800. Since then, every U.S. president, with the exception of George Washington, has resided in the White House. The building has undergone several renovations and expansions over the years to accommodate the evolving needs of the presidency.

In addition to serving as the President's residence, the White House is the center of the executive branch of the U.S. government. It houses the Oval Office, where the President conducts official business, and various rooms for meetings, events, and private quarters for the First Family. The East Wing is often used for official functions, while the West Wing houses the President's staff and offices, including the famous press briefing room.

The White House is not only a symbol of presidential power but also a symbol of the United States as a whole. It is a popular tourist destination, attracting millions of visitors each year who come to see the historic rooms, the beautifully landscaped South Lawn, and the iconic exterior. The White House also hosts numerous official events, such as state dinners, where foreign leaders are welcomed, and important policy announcements are made.

Given its significance, the White House represents more than just a physical residence; it is a symbol of the presidency, American democracy, and the global influence of the United States. The decisions and actions that emanate from the White House have far-reaching implications, making it a focal point for both domestic and international attention.

Here's a thought-provoking query: Which side of the White House is the front? Isn't it confusing by appearance? Unlike traditional buildings with an unmistakable front-facing entrance, the White House challenges observers to discern its primary facade. The question becomes a gateway to a deeper exploration of the structure's layout, revealing layers of historical, ceremonial, and functional considerations. As one examines the intricacies of its design, the ambiguity surrounding the front of the White House unravels, offering insight into its symbolic significance and the multifaceted roles it plays.

On the northern side, facing Pennsylvania Avenue NW, lies the widely recognized front of the White House. This is where the North Portico, adorned with grand columns and a pediment, marks the principal entrance and serves as the backdrop for numerous historical events and official ceremonies. However, the southern side, featuring the South Lawn and the South Portico, offers a contrasting perspective. This area provides a more private and leisurely space, challenging preconceived notions of what constitutes the "front" of such a prominent institution. Ultimately, the White House's intentional design invites contemplation on the nature of symbolism and function, demonstrating that its front is not just a matter of architectural orientation, but a nuanced expression of its diverse roles in American governance.

Capitol Hill

Capitol Hill is a historic neighborhood located in the heart of Washington, the capital city of the United States. It is home to the United States Capitol Building, which houses the chambers of the U.S. Senate and House of Representatives. The area surrounding the Capitol includes office buildings for Members of Congress, such as the Rayburn House Office Building and the Longworth House Office Building.

There are Members of Congress, but those who you will be likely to meet in Washington are Hill staffers, staff who work for members of the US Congress. Hill staffers are ambitious in their carrier dream but toiling their work with low salaries. According to data from LegiStorm, a website that tracks congressional staff salaries, as of 2021 the median salary for House staffers was $59,039, while the median salary for Senate staffers was $65,665.

In addition to the Capitol Building, Capitol Hill is home to many other important government institutions, including the Supreme Court, the Library of Congress, and numerous federal agencies.

The Library of Congress (LOC) in Washington is the world's largest library, established in 1800. It houses millions of books, recordings, manuscripts, and more, with collections spanning diverse subjects. Notable items include the Gutenberg Bible, Thomas Jefferson's personal library, and materials from various U.S. presidents. The LOC is renowned for its commitment to preserving global knowledge. Tourists are drawn to the impressive Thomas Jefferson Building, known for its stunning architecture and the Main Reading Room. Regular exhibitions and events make the LOC a popular destination, reflecting its role as a symbol of knowledge and democracy.

The Supreme Court of the United States (SCOTUS) is the highest judicial body in the country, established by the Constitution. Comprising nine justices, including a Chief Justice, the Supreme Court plays a crucial role in shaping American lives by interpreting the Constitution and settling legal disputes of national importance. Its decisions establish legal precedents that impact various aspects of society, including individual rights, government powers, and social issues.

One notable way the Supreme Court influences American lives is through its rulings on controversial and socially significant issues. Recent rulings on abortion, for example, have had profound effects on reproductive rights. The landmark case of Roe v. Wade in 1973 established a woman's constitutional right to choose to have an abortion, based on the right to privacy. Over the years, the Court has issued decisions that have both expanded and restricted access to abortion services, influencing state laws and regulations.

In recent times, abortion-related cases, such as June Medical Services LLC v. Russo (2020), have attracted attention. In this case, the Court struck down a Louisiana law that required doctors performing abortions to have admitting privileges at nearby hospitals, deeming it an unconstitutional burden on a woman's right to choose. These decisions not only impact the legality of abortion but also contribute to the broader societal dialogue on reproductive rights, healthcare, and individual autonomy.

The Supreme Court's decisions extend beyond abortion, influencing various aspects of American life, such as civil rights, criminal justice, and constitutional interpretation. Its rulings shape the legal landscape and set the course for societal norms and values. As such, the composition of the Court and the appointment of justices become significant political and social events, with nominations and confirmations sparking debates on the direction of constitutional law and the protection of individual liberties. Ultimately, the Supreme Court stands as a central institution in the U.S. legal system, wielding considerable influence over the rights and freedoms of the American people.

The neighborhood is also known for its lively restaurant and bar scene, as well as its cultural institutions, such as the Folger Shakespeare Library and the Eastern Market, a historic public market. Overall, Capitol Hill is a vibrant and dynamic neighborhood that is steeped in history and rich in culture.

Think Tanks

Think tanks are independent and non-profit organizations that conduct research and provide policy-oriented analysis to government, civil society, and the public on a wide range of policy issues. They may specialize in specific policy areas and engage in advocacy and outreach activities to promote their policy recommendations.

You may be wondering why it is important to know about think tanks, as they may seem similar to other research institutes in universities. However, think tanks hold a special significance in Washington for two reasons. Firstly, due to the revolving door practices in Washington, experts from think tanks often transition to positions in the US government. It's important to keep in mind that senior and distinguished fellows you meet today could potentially become Deputy Assistant Secretaries at the Department of Defense in the near future.

Secondly, think tanks are able to thrive in Washington due to its status as a global political city. It's not just the capital of the United States, but also a hub where foreign governments and transnational actors vie to have their voices heard in shaping US foreign policies. Therefore, it's crucial for foreign embassies, multinational companies, and international organizations to work with think tank experts.

As of 2021, there are 398 think tanks in Washington, which is the largest number in the US. Out of the almost 400 think tanks, here's a list of think tanks you need to know.

Center for Strategic and International Studies (CSIS)

The Center for Strategic and International Studies (CSIS), established in 1962 and headquartered in Washington, is a prominent institution dedicated to addressing multifaceted global challenges.

Devoted to in-depth research and analysis, CSIS specializes in international security, economic development, and political affairs. This renowned organization houses various significant programs, each centering on distinct areas of research and analysis to provide comprehensive insights into critical global issues. Among these pivotal programs are the Defense and Security Program, Global Health Policy Center, Energy and National Security Program, International Security Program, and Economics Program.

These diverse initiatives reflect CSIS's commitment to fostering a nuanced understanding of complex global issues and contributing to informed policy discussions on an international scale.

Brookings Institution

The Brookings Institution is one of the most famous

nonprofit public policy organization based in Washington It was founded in 1916 by Robert S. Brookings, a businessman and philanthropist who believed that public policy research and analysis could help improve society.

Brookings conducts research and analysis on a wide range of issues, including economics, foreign policy, governance, and social welfare. Its scholars and experts come from diverse backgrounds and disciplines, including academia, government, and the private sector.

Overall, Brookings is known for its rigorous research and analysis, thereby encouraging its researchers to publish a book as well as monographs.

Center for a New American Security (CNAS)

CNAS is a nonpartisan think tank focused on developing and promoting national security policies for the United States. It was founded in 2007 and is based in Washington

Although CNAS is a nonpartisan think tank and is not formally affiliated with any political party, including the Democratic Party, some of CNAS's scholars and experts have had ties to Democratic administrations and campaigns.

For example, several former Obama admi-nistration officials have served as senior fellows or affiliates of CNAS, including Michèle Flournoy, who was the Under Secretary of Defense for Policy, and John Podesta, who served as Counselor to President Obama. Additionally, several CNAS experts have advised Democratic presidential candidates on national security and foreign policy issues.

Peterson Institute for International Economics (PIIE)

The PIIE is a private, nonprofit, nonpartisan research institution dedicated to the study of international economic policy. It was founded in 1981 by Peter G. Peterson, a former US Secretary of Commerce.

PIIE's mission is to inform and shape public policy debates on international economic issues. Its research focuses on a wide range of topics, including trade, finance, globalization, and international economic cooperation.

PIIE generally supports liberal free trade policies. The Institute's research and analysis often emphasizes the benefits of trade liberalization and globalization, and its scholars and experts have been vocal advocates for free trade agreements and policies that promote greater economic integration among nations.

Council on Foreign Relations (CFR)

The Council on Foreign Relations (CFR) is a nonpartisan think tank based in New York City, with additional offices in Washington and other locations. It was founded in 1921 and is dedicated to promoting understanding of foreign policy and international relations among policymakers, scholars, and the general public.

The CFR is recognized for its significant role in shaping American foreign policy. It achieves this, in part, by publishing the highly respected and influential magazine Foreign Affairs, which focuses on foreign policy and international affairs. Despite its nonpartisan stance, some critics have accused the CFR of being dominated by a "foreign policy establishment" that promotes a particular worldview and set of policy prescriptions.

Heritage Foundation

The Heritage Foundation is a conservative think tank, founded in 1973 by Paul Weyrich and Edwin Feulner with the goal of promoting conservative ideas and principles.

Heritage has been a major influence on conservative policy and Republican politics for decades, but that its close ties to Trump administration once created tensions within the organization. Since then, Heritage and other conservative think tanks and organizations face in navigating the changing political landscape and balancing their role as independent policy researchers with their role as advocates for conservative ideas and policies.

Hudson Institute

The Hudson Institute is a conservative-leaning think tank founded in 1961 by Herman Kahn, a futurist and strategist who specialized in nuclear weapons and military strategy. The institute is named after the Hudson River in New York, near where Kahn lived and worked.

Washington hosts a multitude of policy events each week, ranging from research dissemination to public events. Due to the global pandemic that began in 2020, many think tanks have shifted their events online, allowing for wider participation from individuals regardless of location. However, it is still important to attend events in person to establish valuable networks, which may be one of the reasons why you chose to work in Washington.

Woodrow Wilson International Center for Scholars

The Wilson Center was established in 1968 as a living memorial to the 28th President of the United States, Woodrow Wilson.

The Wilson Center is a public-private partnership and has a unique legal status. It is a nonpartisan institution established by an act of Congress in 1968, and is governed by an independent Board of Trustees appointed by the President of the United States and confirmed by the Senate.

The Wilson Center's unique legal status as a public-private partnership reflects its mission to bridge the worlds of academia and public policy, and to foster dialogue between policymakers, scholars, and the public. This legal structure allows the Wilson Center to maintain its independence and nonpartisan stance while also receiving support from both the government and private donors.

Third Way

The Third Way is recognized as a proponent of modern center-left ideas to the extent that it was once characterized by the New York Times as "radical centrists." Rooted in mainstream American values of opportunity, freedom, and security, the organization identifies itself as center-left, acknowledging this political stance as the most effective means of advancing these ideals in the evolving U.S. political landscape.

Established in 2005 by former Clinton administration staffers, the Third Way firmly believes that the center-left offers the only viable path for the future of the United States. Actively involved in policy research and advocacy, the think tank addresses a range of issues, including climate and energy, the economy, education, health care, national security, and social policy. Notably, Third Way has expressed support for the Women's Health Protection Act, advocating for nationwide access to abortion.

Federal Government Agencies

As the capital city of the United States, Washington is home to a multitude of federal government agencies and institutions. Networking with employees of them is crucial for accessing information, influencing policy, fostering collaborations, navigating regulations, gaining insider insights, achieving professional growth, advocating for causes, discovering job opportunities, facilitating mutual exchange, and engaging in civic responsibilities, all of which collectively enable individuals to stay informed, shape governance, and contribute to the nation's progress on a significant scale.

The three branches of the federal government, consisting of the legislative, executive, and judicial branches, all have a significant presence in Washington. The U.S. Capitol building, located on Capitol Hill, is where the legislative branch, including the House of Representatives and the Senate, convenes to conduct legislative business.

The executive branch, which is responsible for enforcing and carrying out the laws of the land, is housed primarily in the White House and the adjacent Executive Office Building. The departments and agencies that make up the executive branch, such as the Department of State and the Department of Defense, are also located throughout the city.

The Supreme Court, which is the highest court in the United States, is located on Capitol Hill, near the U.S. Capitol building. In addition to the Supreme Court, there are several other federal courts located throughout the city, including the U.S. District Court for the District of Columbia.

In addition to the three branches of government, Washington is also home to numerous federal agencies and organizations, such as the Federal Reserve System and the Environmental Protection Agency. These agencies play an important role in regulating various industries and sectors, and their decisions can have a significant impact on businesses and organizations operating in the city.

The J. Edgar Hoover Building, the current headquarters of the Federal Bureau of Investigation (FBI) in Washington is often characterized by a distinctive but somewhat austere and utilitarian architectural style. Completed in 1975, the building was designed by Charles F. Murphy and Associates in the Brutalist architectural style, a mid-20th-century design characterized by its functional, block-like structures and extensive use of concrete.

The J. Edgar Hoover Building is a large, imposing structure with a precast concrete façade, which gives it a somewhat stark and utilitarian appearance. The exterior features horizontal bands of windows and a grid-like pattern, contributing to the building's robust and fortress-like aesthetics. The design reflects the Brutalist principles of functionality and efficiency, but it has also been criticized for its lack of architectural warmth and visual appeal.

Over the years, the building has faced maintenance issues, and its aging infrastructure has led to discussions about the need for a new facility. Critics of the J. Edgar Hoover Building often point to its concrete-heavy design, small windows, and overall lack of openness, characterizing it as an unwelcoming and dated structure in need of modernization.

The discussions about relocating the FBI headquarters were partly fueled by the desire to provide the agency with a facility that not only addresses security and operational concerns but also presents a more contemporary and inviting image. The potential move could usher in a new era with a modern and technologically advanced headquarters designed to meet the evolving needs of the FBI in the 21st century.

Government Contractors

Government contractors are private companies or organizations that provide goods or services to the United States federal government. These services may include consulting, technology development, construction, logistics, or other specialized services. Government contractors are hired by the government to perform tasks that the government is not equipped to handle in-house.

US Federal Procurement Data System (FPDS), there were approximately 560,000 unique active contractors registered to do business with the US government in the fiscal year 2021. Among them are Lockheed Martin Corporation, Raytheon Technologies Corporation, Booz Allen Hamilton. Quite many government contractors are located in Rosslyn, right across Potomac River from Washington, mostly because Department of Defense, whose biggest bid maker, is located in nearby Crystal City.

Booz Allen Hamilton is a global management consulting firm with a significant presence in the United States. Founded in 1914, the company has grown to become a major player in the fields of management consulting, technology, and engineering services. Booz Allen is known for its work in areas such as cybersecurity, data analytics, artificial intelligence, and government consulting.

The firm has established itself as a key player in shaping government policies, particularly in the United States. Booz Allen has a long history of providing consulting services to various government agencies, including the Department of Defense, intelligence agencies, and civilian government organizations. Its consultants work on a range of issues, from national security and defense strategy to healthcare and infrastructure.

The influence of Booz Allen in shaping government policies stems from its expertise in providing strategic insights, technical solutions, and management consulting services. The firm's consultants often work closely with government officials, offering recommendations and solutions to address complex challenges. Booz Allen's involvement in areas such as cybersecurity and technology consulting has become particularly relevant as governments seek to navigate the rapidly evolving landscape of digital threats and innovations.

It's important to note that while Booz Allen Hamilton is influential in providing expertise and support to government agencies, policy decisions are ultimately made by elected officials and government leaders. Consulting firms like Booz Allen contribute valuable insights and recommendations, but the actual shaping and implementation of policies remain within the purview of government authorities.

Booz Allen's influence also extends beyond the government sector, as it collaborates with private sector clients, non-profit organizations, and international entities. The firm's multidisciplinary approach and diverse range of services contribute to its role as a key player in the broader landscape of management consulting and strategic advisory services.

A substantial presence of government contractors exists in the United States, partly attributed to the trend of successive US administrations since the 1980s aiming for a leaner government and delegating a wide array of functions, ranging from minor to pivotal, to external entities. Former US President Bill Clinton even famously declared in 1996 that "The era of big government is over." As each administration continues this trajectory towards streamlined governance, an increasing number of responsibilities are externalized to private sectors.

In order to secure contracts from both US and foreign governments, these contractors often attend functions, parties, and networking events in Washington, making it likely that you will encounter them in these settings.

International Organizations

Washington is home to many international organizations and institutions. Networking with international organizations in Washington holds significance as it offers a gateway to global diplomacy, collaboration, and cross-cultural understanding. Establishing connections with these organizations provides opportunities to engage in crucial discussions on international affairs, trade, policy, and humanitarian efforts. By fostering relationships with professionals from diverse backgrounds, you can gain insights into global trends, broaden your perspective, and contribute to initiatives that transcend national borders, ultimately playing a pivotal role in shaping global agendas and promoting peaceful cooperation on a worldwide scale.

World Bank Group

The largest international organization in Washington is the World Bank Group. It includes five institutions, namely the International Bank for Reconstruction and Development (IBRD), the International Development Association (IDA), the International Finance Corporation (IFC), the Multilateral Investment Guarantee Agency (MIGA), and the International Centre for Settlement of Investment Disputes

(ICSID).

The International Monetary Fund (IMF)

The International Monetary Fund (IMF) is an international organization that aims to promote international monetary cooperation, facilitate international trade, and promote economic growth and stability. Every April, the World Bank and IMF hold their Spring Meetings, which further increases the already high influx of tourists visiting Washington to witness the cherry blossom season.

The Inter-American Development Bank

The Inter-American Development Bank (IDB) stands as a pivotal force in the realm of multilateral development, channeling its energies toward fostering economic and social progress in the dynamic regions of Latin America and the Caribbean. As a beacon of collaboration and innovation, the IDB endeavors to catalyze positive transformation by providing strategic financial support, fostering sustainable development initiatives, and cultivating partnerships that empower communities and nations to flourish. In its commitment to advancing the well-being of diverse populations, the IDB serves as a catalyst for positive change, enriching the socio-economic fabric of the interconnected nations it engages with.

The Organization of American States

The Organization of American States (OAS) stands as a beacon of regional collaboration, dedicated to enriching the bonds of cooperation and democracy among its member states spanning the vast landscapes of North and South America. This influential organization serves as a dynamic forum where nations converge to cultivate a shared vision of prosperity, human rights, and political stability. Through its tireless commitment to fostering open dialogue and diplomacy, the OAS becomes a crucible for the exchange of ideas and a catalyst for the promotion of democratic values. With a keen focus on inclusivity, the OAS plays a pivotal role in nurturing a hemispheric community where diverse nations can collectively navigate the complexities of governance and forge a path towards a harmonious and democratic future.

Universities

Washington boasts various college and university campuses. Additionally, it serves as a hub for several schools of renowned institutions such as New York University, Texas A&M University, Arizona State, Florida International University, and the University of California system. Notably, the following four universities stand out among them.

George Washington University (GWU)

The main campus of George Washington University is located in the Foggy Bottom neighborhood, offering students close proximity to diverse government institutions, international organizations, and cultural attractions.

Founded in 1821 as The Columbian College in the District of Columbia through an act of Congress, GWU was established with the vision of educating future leaders in government, science, literature, and other fields. Over the years, the university has experienced substantial growth, evolving into a prominent institution at the heart of Washington.

GWU boasts a comprehensive range of undergraduate and graduate programs spanning various disciplines. Notably, the university excels in political science, international affairs, law, business, media, public relations, health sciences, and public health.

The campus life at GWU is dynamic and diverse, providing students with access to a plethora of extracurricular activities, clubs, and organizations. The university actively fosters a vibrant atmosphere through the hosting of various events, guest lectures, and cultural activities, creating a dynamic and engaging environment.

Engaging in cutting-edge research across different disciplines, GWU collaborates with government agencies, international organizations, and industry partners to address pressing global challenges.

Consistently recognized as one of the top universities in the United States, GWU has earned acclaim for its academic excellence, significant research contributions, and its advantageous location in the heart of Washington. It's important to note that rankings may vary depending on the criteria applied, but the university has consistently demonstrated its prominence in higher education.

Georgetown University

Georgetown University, founded in 1789, is a distinguished private research institution located in Washington, renowned for its rich history and unwavering commitment to academic excellence. Situated in the Georgetown neighborhood along the Potomac River, the university's prime location in the nation's capital offers students unparalleled opportunities for internships, research, and engagement with government, international organizations, and cultural institutions.

Chartered by an act of Congress and founded by John Carroll, the first Catholic bishop in the United States, Georgetown University holds the distinction of being the oldest Catholic and Jesuit institution of higher education in the country. Rooted in the Jesuit tradition, the university is dedicated to educating the whole person, emphasizing values such as academic excellence and service.

Despite its esteemed reputation, Georgetown University is known for its relatively high tuition costs, making it one of the more expensive institutions in the United States. The university actively seeks to enhance its campus infrastructure, recognizing the need for expansion. However, the challenge lies in the high cost of real estate in the surrounding neighborhood, posing a financial obstacle to the university's expansion plans.

Georgetown University offers a diverse array of undergraduate, graduate, and professional programs across various disciplines. Notably, its schools of Foreign Service, Law, Business, and Medicine are renowned, with the School of Foreign Service earning particular acclaim for its focus on international affairs.

Fostering a vibrant campus life, Georgetown University places a strong emphasis on community engagement, service, and extracurricular activities. Students are encouraged to actively participate in clubs, organizations, and community service initiatives.

As a Jesuit institution, Georgetown University is guided by values such as service, social justice, and the pursuit of knowledge for the greater good. These principles are seamlessly integrated into both academic and community life.

Despite its tuition being relatively high, Georgetown

University consistently ranks among the top universities in the United States. Its academic reputation, rigorous programs, and dedication to social responsibility contribute to its esteemed standing in both national and international rankings. The university continues to navigate the challenge of expanding its campus within the constraints of the costly surrounding neighborhood.

Johns Hopkins University (JHU)

Johns Hopkins University (JHU), a distinguished private research institution located in Baltimore, Maryland, United States, maintains a notable presence in Washington. Established in 1876 and named after visionary entrepreneur and philanthropist Johns Hopkins, the university has been a trailblazer in integrating teaching and research, earning renown for its unwavering commitment to research and innovation.

JHU's Washington campus stands out for its diverse array of undergraduate and graduate programs, spanning arts and sciences, business, public health, international studies, and more. Notably, the university is esteemed for its significant contributions to science, engineering, health sciences, and its active engagement in international affairs.

Johns Hopkins University's Washington presence is marked by a unique development as its schools and institutions converge into a single building near Capitol Hill on Pennsylvania Avenue in 2023. This centralization, established at the former Newseum building site, cultivates a collaborative environment, promoting interdisciplinary interactions and academic synergy for both students and researchers.

During the pandemic, Johns Hopkins University's hospital played a pivotal role in disseminating credible information about COVID-19. The hospital's announcements regarding the number of COVID-19 cases have been widely recognized as the most credible and authoritative source, contributing significantly to the global understanding of the pandemic's impact.

Beyond academic programs, Johns Hopkins University's affiliation with distinguished medical institutions, such as the Johns Hopkins Hospital and the Johns Hopkins School of Medicine, extends to its Washington campus. These institutions play a crucial role in advancing medical research, enhancing patient care, and shaping the landscape of medical education, further enriching the university's presence in the nation's capital.

Howard University

Howard University, located in Washington, is a private, federally chartered historically black university (HBCU) established in 1867. Named after General Oliver O. Howard, a Civil War hero and commissioner of the Freedmen's Bureau, the university played a pivotal role in providing higher education opportunities for African Americans when access was limited.

As one of the oldest HBCUs in the United States, Howard University is recognized for its commitment to academic excellence. The institution offers a diverse range of undergraduate, graduate, and professional degree programs across various schools and colleges, including the College of Arts and Sciences, the School of Business, the School of Communications, the College of Medicine, and the School of Law.

Throughout its history, Howard University has been a focal point for social justice activism and civil rights movements. Many notable alumni have emerged from the university, contributing significantly to civil rights struggles and other social justice initiatives. Among them is Kamala Harris, the first African American and first Asian American woman to become Vice President of the United States, who graduated from Howard University with a degree in political science and economics.

Situated in the Northwest quadrant of Washington, the university's main campus features a blend of historic and modern buildings, creating a vibrant and intellectually stimulating environment for students.

EXCLUSIVE ENCLAVES OF WASHINGTON: SOCIAL CLUBS

Washington is a city distinguished not only by its iconic monuments and government edifices but also by the presence of exclusive social institutions. These enclaves of privilege contribute uniquely to the social fabric of the nation's capital, acting as repositories of tradition, refinement, and connection. Within their hallowed halls, influential figures from various walks of life converge to shape and participate in the social discourse that defines Washington, making these exclusive clubs an integral part of the city's dynamic identity.

Metropolitan Club

Established in 1863, the Metropolitan Club stands as Washington's oldest and most exclusive private club, embodying a venerable institution exuding refined elegance. Nestled in the heart of the city, its Victorian architecture and opulent interiors narrate the evolving story of Washington over the centuries.

Founded by six US Treasury Department officials, the club's

location near the Department on the corner of H Street and 17th Street has been a constant since its inception. Spanning five stories, the club's interior features a lobby, coat room, card room, a library with an impressive collection of 15,000 books, a grill room, a lounge, a dining room, sleeping quarters, and even a barbershop. Additional facilities include a steam room, an exercise room, and two squash courts, with one room dedicated as a museum honoring the governors.

Positioned as a private club in close proximity to the White House, the Metropolitan Club has been a favored gathering place for politicians and government officials. Notable historical events, such as President Theodore Roosevelt plotting the Spanish–American War and Henry Kissinger regularly meeting with journalists for discussions on current affairs, highlight its significance. To maintain confidentiality during such gatherings, the club strictly prohibits the use of cell phones or note-taking at the tables.

The Metropolitan Club's history includes a transformative shift in its membership policies. For the first century of its existence, the club excluded non-white individuals and did not allow women to join until 1988. In 1961, a significant protest saw thirty members, including Attorney General Robert F. Kennedy, resign in objection. However, in 1972, the club welcomed its first black member, Bishop John T. Walker, marking a crucial turning point in its exclusivity.

A private haven for influential figures, the Metropolitan Club continues to host exclusive events, providing an atmosphere of sophistication that fosters intellectual discourse and social networking among a distinguished membership comprising politicians, diplomats, and business leaders.

University Club

Founded in 1904, the University Club of Washington, D.C., stands as a unique blend of academic and social engagement. Located near Dupont Circle, the club caters to scholars, professionals, and academics, offering an environment where architectural grandeur meets a commitment to intellectual exchange. Hosting lectures, seminars, and cultural events, the club serves as a hub where members engage in thoughtful discussions and cultivate connections across various disciplines.

Launched by sixty-six university and college alumni, the club originated in 1904, initially situated at 1726 I Street, NW. On March 11, 1904, Secretary of War William Howard Taft, an active club member, was elected as its first president. Later, the club moved to its new quarters, a brownstone at

930 Sixteenth Street, NW, with a motto that resonated: "Enter all of ye who have a degree of good fellowship and learning."

In 1936, the University Club merged with the Racquet Club of Washington, relocating to its present location at 1135 Sixteenth Street NW, approximately three blocks north of the White House. The club's facilities include a health and fitness center with two international squash courts, hosting events such as the annual Mosquito Open. Notably, the Tewaaraton Award, the lacrosse equivalent of football's Heisman Trophy, was founded at the club in 2000. Presented annually to the NCAA Lacrosse Player of the Year, the award is jointly presented by The Tewaaraton Foundation and the University Club of Washington.

As of 2022, the University Club's membership dues stand at $3,324 per year for individuals aged 25-29 and $4,488 for those aged 30-34. Additionally, there is a one-time initiation fee of $3,000 at the start of the membership.

Army and Navy Club

Established in 1885, the Army and Navy Club stands as a bastion of tradition, symbolizing a deep-rooted commitment to military heritage and camaraderie. Nestled in the heart of downtown Washington, this institution serves as a haven for military officers, veterans, and esteemed members of the armed forces. Recognized for its historic charm and unwavering dedication to honoring military service, the Army and Navy Club is esteemed as a distinguished gathering place for those who have valiantly served and continue to dedicate themselves to their country.

In its early years, membership to the club was exclusive to officers with wartime service, and it operated from a modest space at the corner of F and 14th streets NW. Over time, the eligibility criteria expanded to include all officers and ex-officers of the Army, Navy, and Marines, fostering a broader sense of camaraderie among military professionals.

In addition to regular membership for officers, individuals closely affiliated with the military profession or distinguished in their respective fields or communities, and who align with the ethos of this Club, may qualify for associate membership. Furthermore, the benefits of membership may be extended to Ambassadors and commissioned officers serving in the armed forces of foreign countries, provided they are currently on duty within the United States.

The Army and Navy Club Library, one of the oldest private libraries in Washington, boasts close to 20,000 volumes, offering an exceptional resource for military history enthusiasts and those seeking the latest developments in the field. This intellectual hub serves as a testament to the club's commitment to preserving and disseminating knowledge within the military community.

Beyond its scholarly pursuits, the club's facilities encompass dining rooms, guest rooms, meeting rooms, squash facilities, and a gym, providing a comprehensive range of amenities to cater to the diverse needs and interests of its distinguished members. The Army and Navy Club, through its rich history and multifaceted offerings, continues to stand as a cherished institution within the military community.

Cosmos Club

Established in 1878, the Cosmos Club is private social club welcoming men and women of distinction in science, literature, the arts, learned professions, or public service. Its magnificent clubhouse, recognized as a District of Columbia Landmark and listed on the National Register of Historic Places, offers a glimpse into the vibrant atmosphere within. The Club's elegant exterior mirrors the richness of cultural and scholarly events hosted within its walls, with members actively engaged in a spectrum of social activities.

The Cosmos Club serves as a historical and prestigious nexus in Washington, uniting individuals from creative, intellectual, and scholarly realms. Since its inception, the Club has fostered camaraderie among some of the greatest minds of our time, boasting a membership that includes presidents, vice presidents, Supreme Court justices, Nobel Prize and Pulitzer Prize winners, as well as recipients of the Presidential Medal of Freedom.

Breaking barriers, the Club granted membership to women in 1988, expanding its inclusivity. The Club's extensive library, a haven for intellectual exploration, reflects its commitment to fostering knowledge and excellence. Members, who are among the brightest in the region, can invite guests, emphasizing the importance of adhering to House Rules and appreciating the Club's architectural heritage.

For those from reciprocal clubs, the Cosmos Club offers luxurious overnight accommodations in the Mansion, the Hillyer House, or the Annex, each stay inclusive of a full breakfast for two. Overnight parking is available on-site for a fee.

Dining options abound at the Club, featuring the Garden Dining Room for breakfast, lunch, dinner (Monday through Saturday), and a monthly Sunday Brunch. The Garden Bar offers an abbreviated menu post-4 pm, complemented by a comprehensive selection of wines and spirits. Additionally, the Club provides various private rooms for hosting dinners, parties, weddings, receptions, and similar events, enhancing its role as a versatile and cherished institution within the Washington social landscape.

FINDING THE PROFESSIONAL DINING EXPERIENCE IN WASHINGTON

Washington boasts numerous gourmet restaurant lists, catering to discerning foodies. If you fall into this category, you may want to skip ahead and consult popular resources such as Yelp, OpenTable, and The Washington Post.

Nevertheless, for professionals, the main purpose of dining out often revolves around socializing. In such instances, it is prudent to seek out a restaurant that provides a cozy and inviting atmosphere, with limited crowds and the option of private rooms, all while offering delectable cuisine.

The Bombay Club (815 Connecticut Ave NW)

The Bombay Club is a popular Indian restaurant among Washingtonians for business lunches and dinners due to its proximity to the White House. The restaurant offers comfortable spacing between tables. If you are having difficulty deciding what to order from the diverse range of Indian dishes, you can opt for Thalis, which is a large platter consisting of an assortment of dishes.

McCormick & Schmick's Seafood & Steaks (1652 K St NW)

This restaurant is a hidden gem, located next to Black Lives Matter Street in Washington, offering a range of options from a power lunch to various fish dishes handpicked by the chef. For a more intimate dining experience, guests can reserve a long table box that can accommodate six to eight people without any additional charge.

Sichuan Pavilion (1814 K St NW)

Sichuan Pavilion stands out among the limited number of authentic Chinese restaurants in Washington. The restaurant is situated in the heart of K Street and serves genuine Sichuan cuisine, such as the famous Mapo Tofu. One corner of the restaurant showcases its rich history of hosting celebrities from the US and China. Although the restaurant can be cramped, with tables situated quite close to each other, I highly recommend it.

Notably, Sichuan Pavilion has also earned the approval of political figures, with both Bush Sr. and Jr. considering it their favorite place for enjoying delectable Sichuan dishes. This endorsement from the two former Presidents adds to the restaurant's prestige and further emphasizes its status as a must-visit establishment in Washington.

Tabard Inn Restaurant (1739 N St NW)

The Tabard Inn restaurant is a popular dining destination located in the historic Tabard Inn hotel in Washington's Dupont Circle neighborhood. The restaurant features American cuisine with a focus on using fresh, seasonal ingredients, and offers a cozy and intimate atmosphere with fireplaces, antique furniture, and unique decor throughout the building.

In addition to its main dining room, the Tabard Inn restaurant also features a bar area, where guests can enjoy a selection of cocktails, beer, and wine, as well as a bar menu with small plates and snacks. The bar area is a popular spot for happy hour, as well as for pre- or post-dinner drinks.

Farmers Fishers Bakers (Harbour at The Georgetown Waterfront, 3000 K St NW)

The Georgetown waterfront is located on the banks of the Potomac River and boasts a spacious public parking lot (Rock Creek Park Trails parking), making it a go-to lunch destination for those coming from Virginia. With many people continuing to work from home post-Covid, this American restaurant is an excellent choice for those looking to meet someone who works remotely from Virginia.

Farmers Fishers Bakers and Founding Farmers are part of the same restaurant group and share a commitment to using locally-sourced and sustainable ingredients in their dishes. Known for their rustic and inviting interior design, both restaurants are popular dining spots with multiple locations throughout the Washington area.

Ocean Prime (1341 G St NW)

Seafood and steakhouse restaurant, known for its upscale atmosphere and high-quality cuisine, making it a popular destination for special occasions and business dinners.

The restaurant offers a menu featuring a range of seafood and steak options, as well as salads, sides, and desserts. Some of the signature dishes include the Chilean Sea Bass, Lobster Mashed Potatoes, and the Prime New York Strip Steak.

Ocean Prime is also a popular destination among international media reporters because of its close proximity to the National Press Building and the White House.

Le Diplomate (1601 14th St NW)

This restaurant is one of the trendiest spots in the city, and its popularity skyrocketed after President Biden stopped by for a French meal with First Lady. The menu offerings are delectable, but be prepared for a crowded atmosphere unless you reserve a table tucked away in a corner. Additionally, finding parking on the street can be a daunting task in Logan Circle, so it's best to leave your car at home when visiting restaurants in this area.

Taberna del Alabardero (1776 I St NW)

Taberna del Alabardero is a Spanish restaurant located in Washington that has been serving traditional Spanish cuisine since 1989. The restaurant offers a range of dishes that reflect the diversity of Spanish cuisine, including paella, tapas, seafood, and a variety of meats.

In addition to its food, Taberna del Alabardero is also known for its atmosphere and decor, which transport diners to Spain with its tiled floors, wooden beams, and rustic charm. The restaurant also offers private event spaces for parties and special occasions, as well as catering services for off-site events. Its tapas dishes are reasonably priced and taste great, so be sure to try them.

Cafe Milano (3251 Prospect St NW)

Café Milano is a reliable choice when seeking a formal setting for important meetings or aiming to make a lasting first impression. Renowned for its refined and elegant atmosphere, the restaurant has become a favored destination for high-profile clientele, drawing in politicians, celebrities, and business leaders alike. The sophisticated ambiance of Café Milano creates a conducive environment for conducting business discussions, sealing deals, or enjoying a memorable meal with an air of exclusivity.

Its menu further enhances its appeal, featuring a diverse range of classic Italian dishes that showcase the culinary excellence of the restaurant. From delectable pasta options to exquisite seafood and meat entrees, each dish is crafted with precision and presented with flair. The menu's highlights include perennial favorites such as the indulgent Spaghetti Carbonara, the rich and flavorful Lobster Ravioli, and the perfectly executed Veal Scallopine, all meticulously prepared with the freshest and finest ingredients. Complemented by an excellent selection of fine wines, Café Milano ensures an unparalleled dining experience where sophistication meets culinary excellence.

Central Michel Richard (1001 Pennsylvania Avenue NW)

Central Michel Richard is a French-American restaurant located in Washington, named after its founder, chef Michel Richard. The restaurant opened in 2007 and quickly gained a reputation as one of the city's best dining establishments, earning a coveted Michelin star in 2016.

The menu at Central Michel Richard featured a blend of classic French dishes and contemporary American cuisine, with an emphasis on high-quality ingredients and creative presentations. Signature dishes included the fried chicken, lobster burger, and "faux" gras (a vegetarian take on foie gras).

The restaurant's location between the White House and Capitol Hill makes it an ideal venue for formal meetings with government officials.

Izakaya Seki (1117 V St NW)

Izakaya Seki stands out among the many Japanese izakayas in the city as one of the few truly authentic Japanese-style pubs, beloved by Japanese expatriates for its small plates and laid-back atmosphere. The restaurant is owned and operated by a family of Japanese immigrants who are passionate about showcasing the best of Japanese cuisine.

Located in the Upper Logan Circle area, Izakaya Seki is not far from other great restaurants and pubs to explore, such as Barcelona Wine Bar and Lupo Verde. So, visitors can make a night of it and enjoy the diverse culinary scene in the neighborhood.

Martin's Tavern (1264 Wisconsin Ave NW)

Martin's Tavern, an enduring gem nestled in Georgetown, Washington, beckons with its historic charm and timeless allure. Stepping through the door, guests are transported to a bygone era, where dark wood finishes and classic ambiance define the interior. Vintage photographs and memorabilia adorning the walls narrate the tavern's rich history since its establishment in 1933. The main dining area, set with white-linen-draped tables and high-backed chairs, bathes in a warm glow, creating an inviting atmosphere that seamlessly marries romance and nostalgia. For those seeking privacy, discreet booths and alcoves offer an intimate retreat, thoughtfully adorned with antique-style lamps and subtle floral touches.

What elevates Martin's Tavern to a realm of historical significance is the booth where Senator John F. Kennedy proposed to Jacqueline Bouvier on June 24, 1953. A discreet plaque commemorates this moment, inviting patrons to share in the history of the very spot where a future President asked for the hand of his beloved. The staff, attired in timeless fashion, provides attentive and gracious service, enhancing the overall experience. Martin's Tavern stands not just as a dining establishment but as a living testament to the intersection of elegance, history, and culinary delight, inviting patrons to savor the ambiance and perhaps create their own momentous memories within its hallowed walls.

EXPLORING ACCOMMODATION OPTIONS IN WASHINGTON

As you navigate your Washington experience, the dynamic nature of the city extends beyond your personal exploration. Washington serves as a magnetic hub, not only for your endeavors but also as a destination drawing friends, family members, colleagues, and fellow nationals to share in your journey. When it comes to accommodating these esteemed guests, the city unfolds a myriad of hotel options, each with its own distinctive narrative and experiential charm.

While you craft your own plan for their stay, consider the array of hotels scattered across the area, each offering a canvas of unique stories and immersive experiences. From historic establishments steeped in the grandeur of the past to modern boutique hotels exuding contemporary chic, Washington's hospitality scene mirrors the diversity and vibrancy of the city itself. These hotels become more than mere accommodations; they become portals into the essence of Washington, providing guests with a taste of the city's history, culture, and dynamic spirit. Whether it's a boutique hotel nestled in a historic neighborhood or a luxury establishment boasting panoramic views of the iconic landmarks, the choices are as varied as the individuals who grace the capital. Thus, in selecting where your guests stay, you not only offer them a place of repose but also an immersive introduction to the multifaceted allure that defines Washington, enriching their visit with memorable tales and experiences unique to this vibrant city.

InterContinental the Willard Washington D.C (1401 Pennsylvania Avenue NW, ★★★★★)

The Willard Hotel is said to be the origin of the term "lobbyist." The term allegedly originated in the 1860s, when President Ulysses S. Grant frequently visited the hotel's lobby to enjoy a cigar and brandy. Politicians and businessmen seeking to influence Grant's administration would often gather in the lobby, waiting to approach him with their ideas and requests. They became known as "lobbyists," named after the hotel's spacious lobby area. The term has since become synonymous with those who seek to influence political decisions.

Waldorf Astoria Washington (1100 Pennsylvania Avenue NW, ★★★★★)

The Waldorf Astoria Washington is a luxury hotel located in the historic Old Post Office building in downtown Washington

Prior to its current name, the hotel was known as the Trump

International Hotel Washington, as it was owned by the Trump Organization. However, after Donald Trump's presidency came to an end, the hotel was sold and was subsequently rebranded as the Waldorf Astoria Washington in 2021.

The building itself, the Old Post Office, was constructed in 1899 and served as the city's main post office for many years. In the 1970s, it was converted into a retail and office space, and it underwent a major renovation in the early 2010s to transform it into a luxury hotel. Today, the Waldorf Astoria Washington remains a popular destination for visitors to the nation's capital.

The Watergate Hotel (2650 Virginia Ave NW, ★★★★★)

The hotel is famously associated with the Watergate scandal of the 1970s, which led to the resignation of President Richard Nixon.

It originally opened in 1967 and quickly became known for its luxurious accommodations and upscale amenities. However, in 1972, a group of burglars were caught breaking into the Democratic National Committee headquarters, which was located in the adjacent Watergate office complex. The ensuing scandal, which involved political espionage and cover-ups, ultimately led to Nixon's downfall and cemented the Watergate Hotel's place in American history.

After years of decline and neglect, the Watergate Hotel underwent a major renovation and reopened in 2016 as a luxury hotel with 336 guest rooms and suites, a rooftop bar and lounge, a full-service spa, and multiple restaurants and event spaces. The hotel's interior design pays homage to the hotel's history with nods to the 1960s and 70s, while also incorporating modern amenities and design elements.

The Hay-Adams (800 16th St NW, ★★★★★)

Nestled at 800 16th Street NW, The Hay-Adams is a five-star sanctuary embodying timeless elegance in downtown Washington. Named after historical figures John Hay and Henry Adams, this hotel, steps away from the White House, seamlessly blends classic charm with modern luxury.

Formerly residences of eminent figures, the hotel boasts meticulously designed rooms and suites, offering a refined retreat. The iconic rooftop terrace provides breathtaking views of the White House and the National Mall, creating an immersive experience amid the city's historical and architectural wonders.

Not only does The Hay-Adams prioritize luxury, but it also champions sustainability, implementing eco-friendly practices for a responsible and conscientious stay. For those seeking a memorable and extraordinary visit to the nation's capital, The Hay-Adams stands as an unparalleled choice, inviting guests to indulge in opulence while immersing themselves in the rich history that surrounds this iconic destination.

Hotel Washington (515 15th St NW, ★★★★)

The Hotel Washington was a historic hotel located in downtown Washington that operated from 1918 to 1973. The hotel was located at the corner of 15th Street and Pennsylvania Avenue, across from the White House, and was a popular destination for politicians, diplomats, and other high-profile guests.

Over the years, the Hotel Washington hosted many important events and guests, including President Franklin D. Roosevelt's inaugural ball in 1941 and the first International Monetary Fund conference in 1946. The hotel was also a popular filming location for movies and television shows, including the 1962 film "Advise and Consent."

The Mayflower Hotel (1127 Connecticut Avenue NW, ★★★★)

Located at 1127 Connecticut Avenue NW, The Mayflower Hotel, part of the Autograph Collection, is a four-star haven blending historic charm with modern luxury in Washington. Since 1925, this iconic hotel has hosted presidents and dignitaries, offering a classic yet contemporary experience.

Rooms and suites at The Mayflower epitomize elegance and functionality, providing a comfortable retreat for guests. The hotel's Palm Court, a verdant oasis, and spa facilities offer relaxation amid the hustle and bustle of the city.

Centrally positioned near Dupont Circle, The Mayflower ensures convenient access to key attractions, making it an ideal choice for both business and leisure travelers. Immerse yourself in Washington's history while enjoying the comforts of this timeless establishment.

Hotel Harrington (436 11th St NW, ★★)

Hotel Harrington is a historic hotel located in downtown Washington. The hotel has been in operation since 1914 and is known for its affordable rates and central location.

The hotel has been in the news recently due to its association with groups such as the Proud Boys, a far-right, anti-immigrant organization. The hotel had previously hosted the Proud Boys during a rally in D.C. in 2018, and again in December 2020, when the group came to the city to support then-president Donald Trump.

Following the events of January 6, 2021, when a mob of Trump supporters stormed the U.S. Capitol building, the hotel faced criticism for its association with far-right groups. As a result, the hotel's owner announced in January 2021 that the hotel would be closing temporarily and undergoing a renovation.

WASHINGTON'S CULTURAL TAPESTRY: ART, MUSIC, AND THEATER SCENE

Just like any other big city, understanding the major schedules and events can help you live a more organized and efficient life. Here are some key highlights to keep in mind.

Art Galleries and Museums

Washington boasts a wealth of artistic treasures housed in its world-class galleries and museums. The National Gallery of Art, divided into the East Building and the West Building, offers a comprehensive journey through art history. From Renaissance masterpieces to modern sculptures, visitors are immersed in a diverse visual feast. The Smithsonian American Art Museum, located in the historic Patent Office Building, showcases an extensive collection of American art, fostering an understanding of the nation's cultural evolution. The Hirshhorn Museum and Sculpture Garden, shaped like a giant donut, presents contemporary and modern art in a unique, circular setting, creating a dynamic visual experience.

The National Portrait Gallery stands as an esteemed

repository of presidential and first lady portraits, capturing the essence of key figures who have played pivotal roles in shaping the American narrative. Housed within the venerable walls of the historic Patent Office Building, the museum is a captivating testament to the art of portraiture and its ability to encapsulate the spirit of leadership. As visitors traverse its halls, they encounter a distinguished collection featuring portraits of U.S. presidents and first ladies, each brushstroke or photograph serving as a visual chronicle of their time in office. With an emphasis on both artistic expression and historical significance, the National Portrait Gallery beckons patrons to explore the nuanced stories embedded in the portraits of these influential figures, ensuring a rich and enlightening experience for all who pass through its doors.

Theatrical Marvels

For those seeking the magic of live performances, the John F. Kennedy Center for the Performing Arts stands as an iconic venue overlooking the Potomac River. This architectural masterpiece, designed by Edward Durell Stone, boasts a distinctive and grand style both inside and outside. The exterior is characterized by its imposing white marble facade and a series of terraced platforms, creating a visually striking and symmetrical appearance. The interior, equally impressive, features elegant and spacious theaters adorned with rich materials and meticulous detailing, providing a luxurious setting for the arts. As patrons step into the Kennedy Center, they are enveloped in an atmosphere that exudes both grandeur and cultural significance.

Within the walls of the Kennedy Center, recent performances have continued to captivate audiences, contributing to the institution's legacy of artistic excellence. One such recent masterpiece was the acclaimed staging of a modern interpretation of a classic ballet, blending traditional choreography with contemporary flair. This innovative performance not only showcased the timeless beauty of the art form but also demonstrated the Kennedy Center's commitment to pushing artistic boundaries and presenting dynamic productions that resonate with diverse audiences. As the Kennedy Center continues to host groundbreaking performances, it solidifies its position as a cultural hub that celebrates the arts in all their evolving forms.

The Kennedy Center, with its unique combination of architectural grandeur and artistic innovation, remains a cultural nexus that transcends time. Its commitment to providing a platform for a diverse range of performances reflects a dedication to enriching the cultural tapestry of Washington. Whether attendees are drawn to the classical elegance of ballet or the dramatic power of theater, the Kennedy Center's majestic setting and unwavering dedication to artistic excellence create an immersive experience that elevates the performing arts to new heights.

Ford's Theatre, forever tied to the tragic history of President

Lincoln's assassination, stands as a multifaceted cultural institution in Washington. Beyond its historical significance, Ford's Theatre has evolved into a dynamic venue that not only preserves the memory of a pivotal moment in American history but also actively contributes to the city's thriving arts scene. The theatre serves as a historical site, where visitors can engage with exhibits and performances that delve into the nation's past. Simultaneously, it acts as a contemporary stage for thought-provoking plays, fostering a dialogue that transcends time. Through its nuanced approach to historical preservation and commitment to the arts, Ford's Theatre emerges as a unique cultural hub that seamlessly intertwines the past and the present.

Located in the Southwest Waterfront, Arena Stage stands as a beacon of innovation in Washington's theatrical landscape. Renowned for its dedication to presenting diverse and socially relevant productions, Arena Stage contributes to the cultural vibrancy of the city. With a commitment to inclusivity, the theatre embraces plays that explore pressing social issues and amplify underrepresented voices. Arena Stage's pioneering spirit extends beyond the stage, reaching into the community to nurture a deeper connection with the arts. Through educational programs, workshops, and community outreach initiatives, Arena Stage not only entertains but also actively engages with the city's residents, fostering a sense of unity and empowerment through the transformative power of theater.

In the pursuit of fostering community arts and contributing to noble causes, Ford's Theatre and Arena Stage share a common commitment to using the stage as a platform for societal reflection and growth. Ford's Theatre, with its historical significance, and Arena Stage, with its contemporary and socially relevant productions, both contribute uniquely to Washington's cultural tapestry. As these theaters continue to play a vital role in the city's artistic scene, they exemplify how the performing arts can serve as a catalyst for both remembrance and progress.

The National Theatre is an enduring symbol of cultural richness and historical significance. Established in 1835, it is one of the oldest continuously operating theaters in the United States, showcasing a legacy that spans nearly two centuries. The theater's architectural grandeur and prime location, situated just a stone's throw away from the White House, add to its allure. Originally conceived as a venue for opera and live performances, the National Theatre has evolved over the years, adapting to changing theatrical trends and technological advancements. Its stage has witnessed a diverse array of performances, from classic plays and Broadway productions to musicals, reflecting the dynamic tapestry of American performing arts. For those fortunate enough, the National Theatre offers an opportunity to savor the magic of Broadway musicals at comparatively affordable prices, ensuring that the captivating allure of live theater remains accessible to a broader audience.

Beyond its architectural and historical significance, the National Theatre has played a crucial role in shaping the cultural landscape of the nation's capital. It has served as a platform for the convergence of artistic excellence and societal dialogue, hosting performances that engage with pressing social and political issues. The theater's commitment to fostering a vibrant arts community is evident through its educational initiatives and outreach programs, which aim to inspire and cultivate the next generation of performers and theater enthusiasts. As a cultural beacon in the heart of Washington, the National Theatre continues to enrich the city's cultural fabric, providing a stage for storytelling that transcends time and resonates with the diverse audiences that grace its hallowed halls.

Musical Odyssey

The rhythmic heartbeat of Washington can be felt in its music scene, and at the center of this melodic tapestry is Blues Alley, the oldest continuing jazz club in the United States. Nestled in the charming streets of Georgetown, this legendary venue has been a cornerstone of the city's jazz culture since 1965. Blues Alley has become an institution where the soulful notes of jazz legends echo through its intimate setting, creating an immersive experience for patrons. With its rich history and commitment to preserving the authenticity of the jazz genre, Blues Alley stands as a testament to Washington's enduring love affair with this timeless musical art form.

This iconic jazz club takes on even greater significance as the epicenter of the annual DC Jazz Festival, held in the heart of the nation's capital. The festival, a celebration of jazz in all its forms, converges on Blues Alley, turning it into a focal point for both local enthusiasts and international jazz aficionados. The intimate venue becomes a hub for diverse performances, showcasing the dynamic range of jazz expressions. From traditional jazz melodies to experimental improvisations, Blues Alley becomes a microcosm of the broader jazz festival, embodying the spirit of creativity and camaraderie that defines the Washington jazz scene. As Blues Alley continues to weave itself into the cultural fabric of the city, it remains a living testament to the enduring legacy and contemporary vitality of jazz music in the United States.

Bohemian Caverns, located in the U Street Corridor, has a rich history dating back to the 1920s, making it a cornerstone of the city's jazz legacy. The Hamilton Live, situated downtown, offers a versatile space hosting everything from jazz and blues to rock and folk, ensuring a diverse musical palette.

Cultural Districts

Beyond individual venues is peppered with cultural districts, each with its own unique character. The U Street Corridor, historically known as "Black Broadway," is a vibrant neighborhood synonymous with jazz and African American culture. Stroll down its streets to find historic theaters, lively music venues, and eclectic boutiques. As the sun sets, the district transforms into a lively hub of activity, especially on Friday and weekend nights. The street scene goes into overdrive, with vibrant energy emanating from the various jazz clubs and music spots that line the corridor.

However, amid the excitement and cultural richness of the U Street Corridor, it's essential to exercise caution, particularly during the heightened activity on weekend nights. As the district comes alive with music and revelry, it also becomes more crowded, and the increased foot traffic may attract opportunistic individuals. Visitors are advised to be mindful of their surroundings and belongings, ensuring a safe and enjoyable experience. While the U Street Corridor is known for its vibrant atmosphere, being aware of the potential for increased activity, especially on weekends, contributes to a well-informed and secure exploration of this dynamic cultural enclave.

Despite the lively and energetic ambiance, it's crucial for visitors to be vigilant and watch out for possible incidents. As the street scene goes crazy with nightlife on Friday and weekend nights, it's not uncommon for incidents like pickpocketing or minor altercations to occur in crowded areas. Being aware of one's surroundings, sticking to well-lit and populated areas, and taking necessary precautions can help ensure a positive experience while exploring the U Street Corridor during its most vibrant hours. By embracing the cultural richness while staying vigilant, visitors can fully enjoy the unique charm and energy that make the U Street Corridor a must-visit cultural destination in Washington.

Dupont Circle, a cosmopolitan area, boasts a blend of galleries, bookstores, and international embassies, creating a dynamic cultural atmosphere. Historically, Dupont Circle was a central gathering area for the LGBTQ+ community, evolving into a vibrant and inclusive neighborhood. While it used to be a hub for gay individuals seeking acceptance and community, Dupont Circle has transformed into one of the most liberal and welcoming areas in Washington. Today, it stands as a symbol of progress and inclusivity, attracting residents and visitors alike with its open-minded atmosphere and diverse cultural offerings.

Within the eclectic tapestry of Dupont Circle, one must not miss the iconic Kramerbooks & Afterwords Cafe. This literary haven, a combination bookstore and café, has been a fixture in the neighborhood since 1976. Kramerbooks offers an extensive selection of books covering a wide range of genres, making it a haven for bibliophiles. Beyond literature, the Afterwords Cafe serves as a gathering place, offering delectable dishes and a cozy ambiance. For those seeking a unique experience, the cafe is not only a great spot for literary exploration but also a place to unwind and enjoy diverse conversations.

As the sun sets over Dupont Circle, the neighborhood transforms into a lively hub of activity. For night owls and those looking for a 24-hour pub experience, The Big Hunt on Connecticut Avenue is a must-visit. This pub, adorned with quirky and artistic decor, remains open around the clock, providing a welcoming atmosphere for patrons at any hour. Whether enjoying a late-night drink, indulging in pub fare, or simply soaking in the eclectic ambiance, The Big Hunt embodies the spirit of Dupont Circle's liberal and lively character, making it an essential stop for those exploring this dynamic neighborhood in the heart of Washington.

WASHINGTON LINGO

Groups, irrespective of their size and composition, often develop their unique slang, fostering a sense of collective identity. Washington is no exception, boasting its own set of distinct lingos intertwined with the city's rich history, iconic buildings, and geographic features. Familiarizing yourself with these expressions is essential for navigating the cultural and political landscape of the nation's capital. Here are some Washington lingos you should be aware of.

Swamp Draining: Referring to efforts to eliminate corruption or bureaucracy, as in "Drain the swamp."

"Swamp Draining" has become a widely used phrase symbolizing a commitment to rooting out corruption and reducing bureaucratic inefficiencies. Coined with the memorable campaign slogan "Drain the swamp," it emphasizes a dedication to bringing about a fundamental change in the political landscape, akin to draining a swamp to eliminate murky elements. This lingo gained prominence as a call for transparency, accountability, and a streamlined government, with proponents aiming to eliminate practices perceived as detrimental to the overall functioning of political institutions. The concept extends beyond the literal act of draining a swamp, embodying a metaphorical commitment to cleaning up and revitalizing the political ecosystem.

Beltway Politics: Describing the political environment within the Interstate 495 beltway surrounding Washington.

"Beltway Politics" encapsulates the unique political culture within the Interstate 495 beltway, a ring road encircling Washington. This term suggests a distinctive set of behaviors, strategies, and perspectives prevalent in the capital's political arena. It often implies a focus on insider dealings, lobbying, and strategic decision-making within this geographical boundary. "Beltway Politics" reflects the notion that Washington operates with its own set of rules, influencing policy discussions and political maneuvering. The term underscores the significance of understanding the dynamics within this specific region to comprehend the intricacies of decision-making and power-brokering in the heart of the nation's political apparatus.

Inside the Beltway: Pertaining to political matters or perspectives originating from within Washington.

"Inside the Beltway" signifies a viewpoint or information source that originates within the geographical confines of Washington. This lingo is often used to describe political insights, discussions, or news that are shaped by the dynamics of the capital city. Being "inside the Beltway" implies an intimate understanding of the intricacies of national politics, policy-making, and the relationships that drive decision-making processes. This term acknowledges the unique perspective that insiders, such as policymakers, lobbyists, and political analysts, bring to discussions and debates on national issues. Understanding the nuances of "Inside the Beltway" discourse is essential for grasping the intricacies of U.S. politics at the highest levels.

The Hill: Referring to Capitol Hill, the home of the U.S. Congress.

"The Hill" is a widely recognized term referring to Capitol Hill, the iconic location housing the United States Congress. As a significant part of Washington, "The Hill" represents the epicenter of legislative power in the country. When used in political lingo, it often denotes the activities, debates, and decisions taking place within the U.S. Congress. Politicians, journalists, and political observers commonly use this term to refer to the hub of legislative activities, and it has become ingrained in the language of Washington, symbolizing the core of American governance.

K Street: Symbolizing Washington's lobbying industry, located on a famous downtown street.

"K Street" is synonymous with Washington's influential lobbying industry. This term refers to a major downtown street in the capital city where many lobbying firms have established their offices. When people talk about "K Street," they are often discussing the nexus of political influence, strategic advocacy, and the complex relationships between corporations, interest groups, and government officials. The term has become shorthand for the broader world of lobbying and the significant role it plays in shaping policy decisions in Washington. Understanding "K Street" is crucial for comprehending the intricate web of connections and interests that impact the policymaking process.

Deep State: Suggesting a hidden, influential network within the government, often associated with bureaucracy.

"Deep State" is a term that implies the existence of a secretive and influential network within the government, operating beyond the visibility of regular political processes. Often associated with elements of the bureaucracy, intelligence agencies, and long-serving officials, the concept of the "Deep State" suggests a continuity of influence that transcends changes in elected leadership. While the term has been used in various contexts, it is frequently employed to describe the perceived resistance or opposition within the government to the agenda of a particular administration. Discussions surrounding the "Deep State" often touch on questions of accountability, transparency, and the balance of power within the government.

The Potomac Two-Step: Describing the political maneuvering and negotiation that takes place.

"The Potomac Two-Step" captures the dynamic and often intricate dance of political maneuvering and negotiation that characterizes the decision-making process in Washington. This lingo emphasizes the strategic steps, compromises, and negotiations undertaken by politicians, lobbyists, and other influencers to navigate the complex political landscape. It suggests a nuanced and sometimes elusive process where individuals must adeptly navigate political currents to achieve their goals. Understanding "The Potomac Two-Step" is essential for comprehending the subtle art of dealmaking and consensus-building within the corridors of power in the nation's capital.

WASHINGTON IN MOVIES AND TV SHOWS

Consider New York, for instance. What impressions does it evoke? Perhaps a sense of luxury, romance, and the cool vibe of city life? Most of these perceptions likely stem from portrayals in movies and TV shows. Now, shift your focus to Washington. Is its image tainted by notions of betrayal and political scheming to destroy enemies? If so, these perceptions, too, are shaped by the visual media you've consumed. Undoubtedly, the portrayal of a city in movies and shows significantly influences its image, making it crucial for us to examine how the capital of the United States is depicted.

Wag the Dog (1997)

Wag the Dog is a political satire film directed by Barry Levinson, hit theaters in 1997 and unfolds against the backdrop of Washington, offering a satirical exploration into the realms of political spin and media manipulation.

The narrative kicks off with a presidential sex scandal surfacing just days before the re-election. To divert public attention from the controversy, presidential aide Winifred Ames (portrayed by Anne Heche) enlists the services of Hollywood producer Stanley Motss (played by Dustin Hoffman) and spin doctor Conrad Brean (embodied by Robert De Niro). Together, their mission is to concoct a fabricated war, strategically designed to serve as a distraction for the public.

Motss and Brean embark on an intricate scheme to manufacture a fictional conflict with Albania. Employing tactics such as staging counterfeit news reports, crafting fabricated war footage, and even composing a patriotic anthem to galvanize public support, their objective is to deftly manipulate public perception. The overarching goal is to present the President as a resolute and commanding leader in the midst of a manufactured crisis.

At its core, the film satirizes the intricate power dynamics between politics and the media, shedding light on the ease with which public opinion can be swayed through meticulously crafted narratives. The title, *Wag the Dog*, cleverly encapsulates the essence of the narrative, symbolizing the manipulation of reality to align with political agendas, where a small event (the tail) controls a larger one (the dog).

Released in December 1997, the film's timing was notably close to the real-life scandal involving President Bill Clinton and Monica Lewinsky. This temporal proximity added an extra layer of impact and relevance, intertwining the fictional narrative with the unfolding events of the time. *Wag the Dog* stands as a thought-provoking commentary on the intricacies of political maneuvering and media orchestration, with Washington, providing the stage for this satirical exploration.

The West Wing (1999-2006, NBC)

The West Wing is a critically acclaimed American television series that originally aired from 1999 to 2006. Created by Aaron Sorkin, the show provides a dramatic depiction of the inner workings of the White House and the lives of the President's staff. The narrative revolves around the fictional President Josiah Bartlet, played by Martin Sheen, and his team of advisors and aides.

Most episodes center around President Bartlet and his team navigating various legislative and political issues. Plots range from discreet negotiations with Congress behind closed doors to personal challenges, such as Josh's struggle with post-traumatic stress disorder in the second season. Typically, episodes loosely follow the President and his staff throughout their day, intertwining several plots connected by a central idea or theme.

The show's unique feature is its expansive, fully connected

set of the White House, enabling producers to capture shots with minimal cuts and long, continuous master shots. This technique, known as "walk and talks," became a signature element of the series. It involves characters engaging in conversations while walking through the hallways, providing a dynamic and immersive experience for viewers.

In the final two seasons, the narrative underwent a shift. The focus of the show divided between plots within the West Wing, featuring President Bartlet and his remaining senior staffers, and storylines revolving around the rest of the main cast on the campaign trail for the 2006 election. This change in perspective added depth and complexity to the overall narrative structure of the show.

In *The West Wing*, Washington is depicted as a place of high-stakes politics, idealism, and the challenges faced by those in power. The show portrays the White House as a hub of intelligence, where witty and fast-paced dialogue reflects the intensity of political decision-making. While the series delves into the complexities of policy and governance, it also explores the personal lives of the characters, providing a more humanizing and relatable aspect to the political landscape.

The depiction of Washington in *The West Wing* is often characterized by a sense of honor and public service, with the characters driven by a genuine desire to make a positive impact on the country. Despite the inevitable political challenges and conflicts, the show emphasizes the importance of principles and ethical decision-making.

Overall, it offers a somewhat idealized portrayal of Washington focusing on the aspirations, dedication, and camaraderie of those working in the highest echelons of government. The series has been praised for its smart writing, compelling characters, and its ability to balance political intrigue with personal drama.

House of Cards (2013-2018, Netflix)

House of Cards is a political drama television series that originally aired from 2013 to 2018. Developed by Beau Willimon and based on a British miniseries of the same name, the show provides a dark and ruthless portrayal of Washington politics. The series follows Frank Underwood, played by Kevin Spacey, a cunning and ambitious politician who, after being passed over for a prestigious appointment, embarks on a relentless quest for power and revenge.

House of Cards follows the Machiavellian rise to power of Frank Underwood, a cunning and ruthless politician in Washington. After being passed over for the position of Secretary of State, Underwood sets out on a vengeful quest to manipulate and exploit the political landscape. Using his strategic prowess, he orchestrates a series of cunning maneuvers, backstabbing allies and enemies alike to ascend the political hierarchy. Alongside his equally formidable wife,

Claire Underwood, played by Robin Wright, Frank engages in deceit, manipulation, and corruption, leaving a trail of shattered lives in his wake. As he climbs the ladder, Frank stops at nothing to secure his influence, even resorting to murder. The series unfolds as a dark and gripping exploration of the morally ambiguous world of politics, where power is the ultimate goal, and ethical boundaries are constantly blurred in the ruthless pursuit of success.

In *House of Cards,* Washington is depicted as a cutthroat and morally ambiguous environment where political maneuvering, manipulation, and corruption are commonplace. The narrative explores the behind-the-scenes machinations of power, revealing the lengths to which characters are willing to go to achieve their ambitions. The show delves into themes of betrayal, loyalty, and the blurred lines between right and wrong in the pursuit of political dominance.

The visual style of the series contributes to the sinister atmosphere, featuring dimly lit rooms, shadowy corners, and intense close-up shots that emphasize the characters' calculated expressions. The depiction of Washington in *House of Cards* contrasts sharply with the idealism portrayed in some other political dramas.

The show not only focuses on political strategy but also explores the personal lives of the characters, revealing the vulnerabilities and flaws that make them both compelling and morally complex. As Frank Underwood climbs the political ladder, viewers witness the erosion of ethical boundaries and the manipulation of individuals and institutions for personal gain.

Overall, *House of Cards* provides a gripping and cynical portrayal of Washington where power is the ultimate currency, and moral compromises are part of the political game. The show has been praised for its compelling storytelling, strong performances, and its unflinching examination of the darker side of politics.

VEEP (2012-2019, HBO)

Veep is a political satire television series that aired from 2012 to 2019. Created by Armando Iannucci, the show provides a comedic and irreverent portrayal of the political landscape in Washington. The main character, Selina Meyer, played by Julia Louis-Dreyfus, begins the series as the Vice President of the United States and later becomes the President. Numerous Hill staff members assert that *Veep* stands out as the most realistic drama portraying the day-to-day realities of politicians and their aides.

Veep follows the political misadventures of Selina Meyer as she navigates the treacherous world of Washington. Starting as the Vice President of the United States, Selina's political journey is marked by a series of comedic blunders, strategic miscalculations, and absurd situations. Alongside her eccentric and often incompetent staff, including Gary Walsh (Tony Hale) and Amy Brookheimer (Anna

Chlumsky), Selina faces the challenges of governance with a mix of sarcasm and ruthless ambition. As she ascends to the presidency, her tenure is plagued by scandals, personal gaffes, and political satire. The show lampoons the self-serving nature of politics, highlighting the absurdity of bureaucracy and the relentless pursuit of power. *Veep* earned acclaim for its sharp humor, clever writing, and Louis-Dreyfus's Emmy-winning performance, providing an entertaining and satirical take on the comedic side of political maneuvering in the nation's capital.

In *Veep,* Washington is depicted as a chaotic and absurd world of bureaucratic ineptitude, political maneuvering, and relentless ambition. The series humorously highlights the trivialities, egos, and absurdities of political life, showcasing the characters' incompetence and self-serving motivations. The show often explores the challenges of governance through a lens of satire, poking fun at the complexities and contradictions inherent in the political process.

Unlike some other political dramas, *Veep* does not focus on the grandiose ideals or moral quandaries of political power but instead revels in the day-to-day absurdities of political life. The dialogue is sharp, filled with profanity-laden humor, and the characters navigate a world where political correctness often takes a backseat to their own personal interests.

The depiction of Washington in *Veep* is characterized by its cynicism and comedic exaggeration, emphasizing the pettiness and trivial nature of politics. The show received acclaim for its witty writing, strong performances, and its ability to find humor in the often dysfunctional aspects of the political arena.

TRANSPORTATION IN WASHINGTON

Transportation in Washington is a dynamic tapestry, offering an array of options to seamlessly navigate the city's vibrant landscape. Whether you're a resident or a visitor, the capital ensures accessibility through its well-connected network.

Air Travel

Washington boasts three major airports catering to domestic and international flights. Ronald Reagan Washington National Airport (DCA), Dulles International Airport (IAD), and Baltimore/Washington International Thurgood Marshall Airport (BWI) provide gateways to the city, ensuring convenient air travel options. Ronald Reagan Washington National Airport, situated just across the Potomac River, is known for its proximity to downtown D.C., making it a favored choice for travelers seeking quick and easy access to the city. With a focus on domestic flights, DCA provides a seamless experience for those flying within the United States, and its strategic location offers breathtaking views of iconic landmarks during takeoff and landing.

Dulles International Airport, named after the United States' 52nd Secretary of State John Foster Dulles, is located in Virginia and serves as a major hub for both domestic and international flights. Recognizable for its distinctive main terminal designed by Eero Saarinen, Dulles offers a unique travel experience. The airport's expansive layout accommodates a multitude of airlines, connecting passengers to destinations worldwide. Dulles International Airport's emphasis on international travel, combined with its state-of-the-art facilities, makes it a prominent choice for those embarking on global journeys. The efficient design and comprehensive amenities ensure a comfortable and streamlined experience for travelers, from check-in to departure.

Baltimore/Washington International Thurgood Marshall Airport, positioned between Baltimore and Washington caters to a diverse range of travelers. Known for its practicality and often favored by those seeking cost-effective options, BWI is a hub for low-cost carriers. Its distance from the city center contributes to its appeal, making it an accessible choice for budget-conscious travelers. Despite its affordability, BWI maintains high standards of service and offers a range of domestic and international flights. The airport's commitment to providing diverse travel options, coupled with its economic advantages, positions it as a valuable asset in the Washington metropolitan area's air travel landscape.

Public Transit

The Washington Metropolitan Area Transit Authority (WMATA) spearheads the city's extensive public transportation system. The Metrorail subway system, with its six color-coded lines, efficiently connects the District of Columbia with Maryland and Virginia suburbs. The Metrobus system, encompassing over 300 routes, including express and limited-stop services, complements the rail network, offering flexibility and convenience.

The WMATA manages the Metrorail and Metrobus services in the Washington, metropolitan area, with a fare structure that considers both distance traveled and time of day. Metrorail fares are based on a six-zone system, and passengers are charged according to the distance covered. Peak and off-peak rates apply during designated times, with peak fares in effect during weekday rush hours. The Metrobus system generally employs a flat-rate fare structure, with charges applying per boarding. Utilizing a contactless smart card called SmarTrip is the standard method of fare payment for both Metrorail and Metrobus. SmarTrip cards facilitate entry and exit at Metrorail stations and streamline boarding on Metrobuses. Additionally, discounted fares are available for seniors and persons with disabilities, and children under five can ride for free when accompanied by a fare-paying adult.

In 2022, the District of Columbia Council proposed the idea of making WMATA bus services fare-free within the District starting the following year. Charles Allen, the creator of the Metro for D.C. bill and Councilmember for Ward 6, along with Council Chair Phil Mendelson, announced during a press conference that the implementation of this fare-free service would require $32 million in funding. The plan aimed to allow passengers boarding buses at any of D.C.'s 10,000 bus stops to travel for free, eliminating the need for the usual $2 fare, even if their journey extended into Virginia or Maryland.

However, as of 2023, there has been no progress on this initiative. The Metro Board of Directors has requested the D.C. Council to postpone, by a year, the plan to make Metrobuses free of charge within the city limits. This setback represents a challenge to an initiative that had gained popularity among lawmakers but had encountered various obstacles and objections.

Trains

Union Station in Washington is a significant hub for Amtrak, facilitating both long-distance and regional train services. Amtrak offers convenient rail connections to cities along the East Coast, the Midwest, and various regions across the United States. For instance, a trip from Union Station to New York takes only three and a half hours, with ticket prices ranging between $30 and $70 for a one-way journey. This presents a notable advantage over bus trips in terms of both time efficiency and convenience. However, it's worth noting that regional trains may experience more delays compared to the high-speed Acela service.

Opened in 1907, Union Station is not just a transportation hub but an architectural masterpiece. Designed in the

Beaux-Arts style, it boasts a grand interior with a cavernous main hall characterized by soaring ceilings, ornate decorations, and majestic columns. The detailed craftsmanship, including intricate moldings, decorative carvings, and a captivating blend of classical and neoclassical elements, contributes to its timeless elegance.

The exterior of Union Station is equally impressive, featuring a monumental facade adorned with classical sculptures and intricate detailing. The station's facade and clock tower evoke a sense of grandeur and historic significance, making it a recognizable landmark in the nation's capital.

While Union Station has a rich history and architectural significance, it's important to be cautious when visiting. In recent times, the station has experienced a decline in its peak crowd levels, and there have been reports of increased presence of homeless individuals and individuals struggling with addiction issues. Visitors are advised to exercise extra care and awareness when navigating the surroundings.

Ride-Hailing and Taxis

Taxis and ride-hailing services, including Uber and Lyft, are ubiquitous in the city, providing a convenient alternative for personalized transportation tailored to your schedule and destination.

The cost of a ride is influenced by several factors, including the base fare, per-mile rate, per-minute rate, and any applicable booking fees. These variables contribute to the overall expense of a ride within the city, where prices can vary based on the distance traveled, time of day, and demand for rides.

For trips from Washington to nearby areas like Arlington, Virginia, the cost typically falls within the range of $15 to $25. However, these estimates are subject to change, and factors such as surge pricing during periods of high demand can impact the final fare. For rides extending beyond state lines, passengers can expect higher costs, and additional fees may apply. To obtain the most up-to-date and accurate pricing information, passengers are advised to check the respective ride-hailing apps or websites before booking a ride.

Driving

Washington accommodates those who prefer the autonomy of driving with an intricate network of highways and bridges providing access to the city. However, it's important to note that traffic can be dense, particularly during rush hours. Washington experiences dense traffic during rush hours, primarily influenced by its status as the capital of the United States, the concentration of government offices, and the presence of diplomatic missions and businesses. The morning rush typically spans from 7:00 AM to 9:00 AM, while the afternoon rush occurs around 4:30 PM to 6:30 PM. Major arteries such as I-395, I-495 (the Capital Beltway), I-66, and key urban routes like K Street and Connecticut Avenue often face heavy congestion. Despite efforts to improve public transportation options, including the Washington Metropolitan Area Transit Authority (WMATA) services, the city's layout, ongoing urban development, and a growing population contribute to the ongoing challenge of traffic congestion during peak hours. Real-time traffic updates and local reports provide essential information for navigating Washington's busy roadways.

Street parking is available, although it may be limited, with certain areas requiring permits or adhering to time restrictions. Street parking can be particularly challenging in the downtown or central business district, especially during business hours, due to the high demand for limited parking spaces. Tourist hotspots like the National Mall, the U.S. Capitol, and the White House, as well as lively neighborhoods such as Georgetown and Adams Morgan, also experience heightened competition for street parking, especially during evenings and weekends. Given the limited availability and the complexities of parking regulations, visitors and locals alike are often advised to explore alternative options such as parking garages or utilizing public transportation in these bustling areas.

Paid parking garages and lots are strategically placed throughout the city, offering convenience for those choosing to explore the capital by car. Garage parking is a widely utilized option due to the complexities of street parking in busy areas. Rates for garage parking vary based on factors such as location and time of day. In the downtown or central business district, hourly rates can range from $10 to $20 or more, with daily rates exceeding $30 or $40. Popular tourist areas near the National Mall or U.S. Capitol may also have higher rates, often exceeding $20 for a few hours. Neighborhoods like Georgetown or Adams Morgan offer garage parking with hourly rates, and daily maximums typically range from $15 to $30 or more. Event-specific pricing may apply during major events, and for regular users, monthly parking passes are available at varying rates, typically ranging from around $150 to $400 or more, depending on the location and amenities. It's advisable to check specific garage rates and hours, as they may have changed, and utilizing parking apps or websites can provide real-time information on available spaces and pricing.

Electric Micromobility

Washington has embraced a new wave of urban mobility: e-bikes and e-scooters. These zippy little vehicles are transforming the way residents and visitors navigate the city, offering a fun, sustainable, and often faster alternative to cars or public transportation.

With multiple e-bike and e-scooter rental companies like

Lime, Bird, and Veo operating in the city, finding a ride is not difficult. Download their apps, locate a nearby vehicle, and be on your way in minutes.

In 2024, Lime, the San Francisco-based micromobility company, announced a launch of its next-generation electric bikes. Lime's $50 million investment in a major e-bike expansion is now materializing as the company introduces its improved bikes in the North American market, starting with Washington.

As E-micromobility spreads every corner of Washington, it isn't just about getting around. It is about connecting with the city and its communities. You can join group rides organized by local clubs or simply strike up conversations with fellow riders along the way. You'll be surprised at the sense of camaraderie and shared exploration that e-bikes and e-scooters foster.

But, remember, even though e-bikes and e-scooters are a blast, safety is paramount. Always wear a helmet, follow traffic rules, and be mindful of pedestrians and other riders. Familiarize yourself with the city's regulations, like designated parking zones and no-ride areas.

ADDITIONAL TIPS FOR YOUR QUICK SETTLEMENT

Just like any other big city, understanding the major schedules and events can help you live a more organized and efficient life. Here are some key highlights to keep in mind.

Be aware of Washington Annual Calendar

Everyday

Keep in mind that Washington is a city where VIPs reside and visit regularly. As a result, you may encounter blaring police sirens when the vice president heads to work or the president moves in and out of the White House, along with foreign dignitaries visiting the city. However, the presence of numerous police and secret service forces patrolling the downtown area contributes to a heightened sense of security, making Washington comparatively safer than other major cities in the United States.

Moreover, Washington's cultural scene is an aspect that you should fully embrace in your daily life. There are numerous world-class museums and institutions, many of which are part of the Smithsonian Institution. One remarkable aspect is the accessibility to these museums for free. The Smithsonian Museums, including the National Museum of American History, the National Air and Space Museum, and the National Gallery of Art, among others, offer free admission to visitors, making cultural exploration accessible to everyone.

The Smithsonian Institution, often referred to as "America's attic," houses an extensive collection of artifacts, artworks, and exhibits that span diverse disciplines such as history, science, art, and culture. The National Mall is home to several iconic Smithsonian museums, creating a unique cultural corridor that attracts millions of visitors each year.

Beyond the Smithsonian, Washington boasts a vibrant arts scene with numerous galleries, theaters, and performance spaces. The John F. Kennedy Center for the Performing Arts hosts a variety of world-class performances, from ballet and opera to theater and musicals. The city is also home to the Shakespeare Theatre Company, providing classical and contemporary theater productions.

Cultural events and festivals further contribute to the city's dynamic cultural life. The National Cherry Blossom Festival, the Smithsonian Folklife Festival, and the H Street Festival are just a few examples of the diverse and celebratory events that take place throughout the year.

Moreover, Washington is steeped in history, with iconic landmarks such as the Washington Monument, the Lincoln Memorial, and the U.S. Capitol serving as not just physical structures but also symbols of the nation's heritage. The city's rich history is showcased not only in its museums but also in its architecture, monuments, and the overall layout of the city.

January – Congress beginning

When Congress begins its session in January each year, there is a sense of anticipation and activity in the Capitol Building. Newly elected and returning members gather, taking part in formal ceremonies and speeches to outline their legislative goals.

During this time, the halls of Congress are bustling with preparations for the upcoming legislative agenda. Committees meet, bills are drafted, and bipartisan interactions are evident as lawmakers come together to work towards common goals. The media and public attention are heightened as the nation watches closely for the progress and challenges that lie ahead. Overall, the opening days of Congress symbolize a fresh start, where elected representatives demonstrate their commitment to serving the country and finding solutions to the issues facing the nation.

April – Cherry Blossom Festival

In April, Washington, can experience varying levels of crowds depending on the specific events and activities taking place during that time. The National Cherry Blossom Festival is a significant event that usually takes place from late March to early April. During this time, the city experiences a surge in visitors who come to witness the iconic cherry blossoms in full bloom around the Tidal Basin and other locations. This festival attracts both domestic and international tourists, leading to higher-than-usual crowds during this period.

In Washington, there are several spots offer enchanting views of these delicate blooms. The Tidal Basin is perhaps the most iconic location, with thousands of cherry trees lining its shores. As you stroll along the basin, you're treated to breathtaking vistas of the blossoms against the backdrop of the Washington Monument and Jefferson Memorial. The National Mall, flanked by the Lincoln Memorial and the U.S. Capitol, is another prime location, providing a grand setting for cherry blossom appreciation. The Reflecting Pool adds to the allure, creating a serene atmosphere for both locals and visitors.

For a more secluded experience, venture to East Potomac Park, located on Hains Point. This lesser-known spot offers a tranquil setting with cherry trees lining the waterfront, providing a peaceful escape from the crowds at the Tidal Basin. Additionally, Kenwood in Bethesda, just outside the city, is a charming residential neighborhood known for its picturesque streets adorned with cherry blossoms. It offers a more intimate and residential perspective on the beauty of the blooms.

If you prefer a broader landscape for cherry blossom viewing, the United States National Arboretum is an excellent choice. The arboretum features a diverse collection of cherry blossoms dispersed throughout its expansive grounds. Lastly, Dumbarton Oaks in Georgetown provides an elegant setting with gardens showcasing cherry blossoms. As you explore these different locations, keep in mind that the peak bloom period can vary yearly based on weather conditions, so it's advisable to check updated information for the best timing to witness this spectacular display.

May – Embassy Open Houses

Washington's embassy open houses in May, known as "Passport DC" or "Around the World Embassy Tour," offer a unique cultural experience for visitors. Held annually as part of International Cultural Awareness Month, numerous foreign embassies open their doors to showcase their country's heritage, traditions, and cuisine. Participants can explore stunning embassy buildings, enjoy art exhibitions, cultural performances, and engage with diplomats and staff to learn more about various nations. The event fosters intercultural understanding, celebrates global diversity, and promotes diplomatic connections, creating a vibrant and enriching atmosphere in the heart of the nation's capital.

The embassy open houses in May on Embassy Row provide a captivating and educational journey into different cultures. With engaging performances, demonstrations, and culinary delights, attendees immerse themselves in a diverse array of experiences. This annual celebration unites people from all backgrounds, offering a shared appreciation for cultural richness and diplomacy while promoting a deeper understanding of the world's cultures. It is a remarkable opportunity for locals and tourists alike to celebrate the beauty of global diversity in the lively and welcoming atmosphere of Washington's embassy community.

July – Independence Day Fireworks

On Independence Day, Washington hosts a thrilling and patriotic celebration with a spectacular fireworks display. The city comes alive with a sense of national pride as locals and visitors gather to witness the festivities. Throughout the day, people enjoy the National Independence Day Parade, featuring marching bands, military units, and community groups showcasing American history and culture. As the evening approaches, crowds converge on the National Mall to secure the best spots for the fireworks show. At around 9:00 PM, the night sky above the iconic Washington Monument is illuminated with a breathtaking array of colors and patterns, synchronized to patriotic music. The electrifying atmosphere, shared sense of unity, and stunning visual spectacle make the Independence Day fireworks in Washington an unforgettable and cherished experience for all who attend.

To ensure a memorable experience witnessing the July 4th fireworks in Washington, strategic planning is key. Arriving early is crucial, as the nation's capital attracts large crowds on Independence Day. Opt for prime viewing spots such as the National Mall or consider alternative locations along the Potomac River for a slightly less congested experience. Bring essentials like water, snacks, sunscreen, and comfortable seating, as well as a picnic setup to enhance your celebration. Be mindful of security regulations, as heightened measures may be in place. Utilize public transportation, as parking can be challenging, and stay weather-prepared with appropriate clothing and hydration. Planning an exit strategy in advance will help navigate the crowds efficiently.

For those seeking a more relaxed experience, exploring alternative viewing options is worth considering. Some hotels, rooftop bars, or boat cruises may offer unique vantage points for the fireworks. These alternatives provide a more intimate setting while still allowing you to partake in the festive atmosphere. Whether you choose the iconic National Mall or an off-the-beaten-path location, careful planning will contribute to a smoother and more enjoyable Independence Day celebration in the heart of the nation's capital.

September – Enjoy Autumn

In September, Washington embraces the arrival of fall with a variety of events and activities. One highlight is the National Book Festival, an annual celebration hosted by the Library of Congress on the National Mall. This literary extravaganza brings together renowned authors, illustrators, and book enthusiasts for presentations, panel discussions, and book signings. It's a fantastic opportunity for literary lovers to engage with their favorite writers and discover new voices in the literary world.

Museum enthusiasts can take advantage of Smithsonian Magazine's Museum Day, usually held in September. Participating museums across the city open their doors for free, allowing visitors to explore the rich cultural and historical heritage housed in these institutions. It's a chance to dive into art, science, history, and more, all while enjoying complimentary admission.

For those seeking a vibrant street festival experience, the H Street Festival is a must-attend event. Taking place on H Street NE, this annual celebration showcases the neighborhood's diverse culture with live music, food vendors, art displays, and a lively atmosphere. It's a family-friendly event that provides a taste of the local community's creativity and energy.

Sports enthusiasts can catch the excitement of Major League Baseball as the Washington Nationals play their home games at Nationals Park. September marks the end of the regular season, making it an opportune time to experience the thrill of a live baseball game. Whether you're a literary enthusiast, museum-goer, festival lover, or sports fan, Washington in September offers a diverse array of activities to suit various interests.

December – Christmas

The Christmas season in Washington, transforms the city into a festive wonderland, filled with enchanting lights, decorations, and holiday spirit. As December approaches, iconic landmarks, such as the National Christmas Tree near the White House and the Capitol Christmas Tree, are beautifully adorned with colorful lights and ornaments, creating a magical ambiance. The National Mall is aglow with festive displays, and many of the city's neighborhoods boast elaborate decorations on houses and storefronts. Visitors and locals alike can enjoy various holiday-themed events, from Christmas markets and ice skating rinks to seasonal concerts and theatrical performances. The city's museums and attractions also join in the celebration, offering special holiday-themed exhibits and activities for families and tourists. The Christmas season in Washington, is a time of joy, togetherness, and celebration, making it a captivating destination for all who want to experience the magic of the holidays.

Beyond the dazzling decorations, Washington's Christmas season offers heartwarming traditions and ceremonies. The National Christmas Tree Lighting Ceremony, attended by dignitaries and performers, marks the official start of the holiday season, spreading warmth and cheer across the nation. The city hosts numerous festive parades, including the Downtown Holiday Market and the National Hanukkah Menorah Lighting, celebrating the diversity of holiday traditions in the capital. Visitors can take part in seasonal activities like carriage rides through illuminated streets or indulge in holiday treats from the city's many bakeries and restaurants. Throughout December, residents and visitors enjoy the enchanting atmosphere as the city comes alive with holiday-themed events, creating cherished memories and fostering a sense of unity during the most wonderful time of the year.

Navigating Information Highways: newsletters, local media, and SNS

Twitter (X, Now)

Contrary to popular belief, Twitter remains a powerful tool for individuals looking to engage with policy experts and stay up-to-date with the latest developments in their fields, particularly in Washington. With its 140-character limit, Twitter allows for quick and easy dissemination of information and has become a go-to platform for policy wonks and thought leaders in the capital city.

If you plan to work or operate in Washington, it is advisable to reactivate and revamp your Twitter account. By following relevant policy experts and thought leaders in your areas of interest, you can stay informed about the latest policy debates, emerging trends, and breaking news.

One of the advantages of Twitter is its ability to connect

individuals with a diverse range of users, many of whom they may not have encountered otherwise. By following a few experts in your field, you can expand your network and potentially make new connections that can advance your career or professional goals.

In addition to its networking benefits, Twitter also offers a unique platform for individuals to share their thoughts and ideas with a broader audience. Through the use of hashtags and other tools, users can join ongoing conversations and contribute their insights to important policy debates.

Newsletters

Subscribing to newsletters from think tanks, international organizations, law firms, and lobby groups is highly recommended. As information is crucial in Washington, these newsletters provide rich insights into policy, political, and foreign affairs, among other goings-on in the capital city.

Many organizations and think tanks in Washington offer free events, such as panel discussions, roundtables, and lectures, that cover a wide range of topics such as politics, economics, national security, and international relations. By subscribing to these newsletters, you can stay up-to-date on the latest events and attend those that are most relevant to your interests. Not only can these events expand your knowledge and understanding of key issues, but they can also provide valuable networking opportunities with experts and professionals in your field. Therefore, it's highly recommended to take advantage of these resources and stay informed about the various events and happenings in the DC area.

Happy Hours

Networking is crucial in D.C. because it is a city built on relationships. In a town where who you know matters, cultivating a strong network can provide opportunities for career advancement, access to valuable information, and potential collaborations. In addition to attending events and happy hours, it's important to seek out mentors and connect with colleagues in your field. Building strong relationships takes time and effort, but it can pay off in numerous ways. Remember, the connections you make in D.C. can benefit you both personally and professionally for years to come.

Attending in-person happy hours can be a great way to expand your network in Washington Many networking events, happy hours, and functions are hosted by policy institutes, embassies, companies, and the U.S. government. If your schedule permits, be sure to join these events as you never know who you might meet. It can be a fruitful experience that could lead to valuable connections.

ABOUT THE AUTHOR

Jayeel Munch is a seasoned professional with an extensive career spanning the governmental sector and international organizations, having dedicated his expertise to over 10 cities throughout his entire professional journey. Munch's wealth of experience has been cultivated through years of meaningful contributions in various locations worldwide. Currently, he is channeling his passion for storytelling into the creation of his "professional city dwellers series." This ongoing project encapsulates the cities where he has not only worked but also lived and cherished significant life experiences. Through his writing, Munch aims to capture the essence of each city, weaving together a narrative that reflects his professional growth, personal connections, and the unique cultural tapestry that has shaped his life thus far. As he delves into the intricate details of his journey, Munch invites readers to join him in a reflective exploration of the diverse landscapes that have left an indelible mark on his professional and personal narrative.

Made in United States
North Haven, CT
16 May 2025

68928281R00079